For the Gods of Girsu
City-State Formation in Ancient Sumer

Sébastien Rey

Archaeopress Archaeology

Archaeopress Publishing Ltd
Gordon House
276 Banbury Road
Oxford OX2 7ED

www.archaeopress.com

ISBN 978 1 78491 389 2
ISBN 978 1 78491 390 8 (e-Pdf)

© Archaeopress and Sébastien Rey 2016

Cover illustration: Archaic bas-relief of the *Figure aux plumes*
(© Musée du Louvre, Dist. RMN-Grand Palais, P. Fuzeau)

All rights reserved. No part of this book may be reproduced, stored in retrieval system,
or transmitted, in any form or by any means, electronic, mechanical, photocopying or otherwise,
without the prior written permission of the copyright owners.

Printed in England by Oxuniprint, Oxford

This book is available direct from Archaeopress or from our website www.archaeopress.com

Contents

List of Figures ii

Foreword iii

Preface v

Introduction: Concept of the Sumerian City-State 1

Chapter One: Once Upon a Time in Ancient Girsu. Or Tello and the Rediscovery of the Sumerians 5
    Tello/Girsu and the Sumerian Miracle 5
    The Myth of the Archaic Temple-City 12
    Primitive Democracy or Polyarchy? 13
    Standing in the Shadows of Giants 14

Chapter Two: The City of the Heroic God. The General Layout of a Sumerian Metropolis 15
    A Landscape of Spoils as a Legacy of the Pioneers 15
    Moving Landscapes and the Power of Space Imagery 17
    Multivallation for the Purpose of Coercion and Defense 20
    The Ceremonial Landscape of the City-State's Pantheon 25
    The Logistical Infrastructure of the Ancient Waterways 31

Chapter Three: The Girsu Countryside. The Spatial Organization of a Sumerian City-State 37
    The Myth of the Sumerian Archaic Agrotown 37
    The Regional Setting of an Early Dynastic City-State 39
    The Ritual Processions in Honor of the Gods 45
    The Sacred Precinct and Central Cult of the City-State 47

Chapter Four: Demarcated by the Gods. Sumerian Rites and the Lagaš-Umma Border Conflict 53
    The Sumerian Concept of Sacred Territoriality 53
    Contextualizing the Lagaš-Umma Border Conflict 54
    Characterizing the Presargonic Gu'edena frontier 60
    The Rise of the Mesopotamian Imperial State 64

Conclusion: Morphogenesis of an Archaic City-State 67

Bibliography 71

List of Figures

Fig. 1: The Tower of Babel by Bruegel the Elder 6
Fig. 2: Ernest de Sarzec and his escort at Tello 8
Fig. 3: Apotropaic pillar composed of inscribed bricks from Gudea 8
Fig. 4: Stele of the Vultures. Mythological side 9
Fig. 5: Spatial organization of the sacred precinct of Girsu 11
Fig. 6: The central complex of mounds of Tello (Tell K, Tell I-I') 16
Fig. 7: 1968 Corona space photography of Tello 18
Fig. 8: Principal topographical features and quarters of ancient Girsu 20
Fig. 9: Schematic plan of the Early Dynastic defended gate of the mound of the *Porte du Diable* 22
Fig. 10: Schematic plan of the Early Dynastic religious complex of Ningirsu 26
Fig. 11: Mace of Me-salim of Kiš recording the earliest known ruler of Lagaš Lugal-ša-engur 27
Fig. 12: Artistic view of the Early Dynastic temple of Ningirsu 30
Fig. 13: The so-called Enigmatic construction of the Eastern tells, in fact a bridge over a paleo-channel 32
Fig. 14: Modern high resolution space photography of Tello 33
Fig. 15: General layout and topographical features of the Early Dynastic religious megapolis of Girsu 36
Fig. 16: The immediate hinterlands of Girsu 38
Fig. 17: 1968 Corona space photography of Southern Babylonia 43
Fig. 18: Map of the Early Dynastic settlement pattern of the Girsu-Lagaš city-state 44
Fig. 19: Map of the Early Dynastic network of watercourses and marshlands 45
Fig. 20: Reconstruction of the Early Dynastic ritual procession-ways of the Girsu-Lagaš city-state 47
Fig. 21: General view of the sacred precinct of Girsu (November 2015) 48
Fig. 22: The Early Dynastic ceremonial plaza of the sacred precinct of Girsu 50
Fig. 23: Early Dynastic III ceremonial terracotta vessels from Area A 51
Fig. 24: The Early Dynastic Sumerian alluvium featuring the Gu'edena frontier 55
Fig. 25: Stele of the Vultures. Historical side 59
Fig. 26: Reconstruction of the Lugal-zagesi campaign against Lagaš 65
Fig. 27: Archaic bas-relief of the *Figure aux plumes* 68

Foreword

It gives me particular pleasure to introduce this volume on the site of Tello, ancient *Girsu*, in southern Iraq. Not only is Tello surely one of the most important ancient Mesopotamian sites in its own right, but it also provides the field focus for an outstanding initiative of the British Museum, designed to build capacity in the Iraq State Board for Antiquities and Heritage (SBAH) during a period of conflict in the region. Termed the Iraq Emergency Heritage Management Training Scheme, the programme, which began in April, 2016, is intended to provide intensive training to Iraqi heritage professionals in all of the retrieval and documentation skills and techniques they will need in order to confront the challenges of severely disrupted and substantially damaged archaeological sites when such sites are liberated from the hands of those who would seek to destroy them and are returned to effective and stable governmental control. The scheme, run partly in the UK, and partly in the field in Iraq at sites agreed in association with the SBAH, necessitated the engagement to the British Museum's staff of two senior field archaeologists, both to lead the training in the UK and to direct the field seasons in Iraq. I was delighted, therefore, when Sebastien Rey, an internationally acknowledged expert on Mesopotamian archaeology and an experienced excavator, was appointed to one of these key positions.

Sebastien has brought to the BM, not only his extensive knowledge and expertise, but also the permit to conduct excavations at Tello, a project he began in 2015 together with his Iraqi colleague, Fatma Husain. One could not wish for a more appropriate site at which to provide field training for our Iraq Scheme participants, but, beyond that, one could not wish for a more significant site at which to further explore the many and varied aspects of Sumerian civilization.

The 2015 season marks a return to Tello for the purposes of excavation after a gap of some 82 years. The first campaign undertaken by the French vice-consul in Basra, Ernest de Sarzec began in 1877 and represented the first ever exploration of a Sumerian site in Iraq. Continuing until 1900, Sarzec's discoveries, particularly of a hitherto totally unknown style of statuary, caused a sensation when presented to Paris audiences in the 1880's. Subsequent campaigns of excavations, all undertaken by eminent French scholars, concluded in 1933, by which time the combined total of field seasons amounted to twenty. From the results of the various investigations, a considerable amount of information had already been obtained about Tello before Sebastien returned to the site in 2015. Its identification as ancient *Girsu* was assured on the basis of epigraphic finds, as too was its role as one of the most important cities of the Sumerian state of Lagash, and for a time, the state capital. The early excavations uncovered a number of impressive religious complexes as well as thousands of cuneiform tablets which document all aspects of the city-state's social, political, economic and religious institutions. Many of Tello's impressive finds are displayed in museums around the world, including indeed the British Museum. With all that is known, It would not be unreasonable, perhaps, to question the need to resume excavations at such an apparently well-explored site, but in answer, it must be remembered that all of the previous campaigns took place well before the development of appropriate, scientifically-controlled and systematically rigorous excavation techniques, with the result that much of the information recovered is either unrecorded or imprecisely documented, and many of the finds lack contextual precision. None of these failings apply to Sebastien's new excavations which, over the coming years, will undoubtedly set the standard for fieldwork methodology in Iraq.

This book, which summarizes everything that is known of Tello from previous work, and records the results of the initial 2015 season of excavations, sets the scene for the more extensive field seasons to follow. I am indebted to Sebastien for bringing this wonderful site to the British Museum, and for producing this excellent volume to highlight its enormous significance.

Jonathan N. Tubb
Keeper, Middle East Department
The British Museum

Preface

After 20 pre-World War II archaeological seasons and following an interruption of 82 years of fieldwork, I had the honor in 2015, together with co-director Fatma Husain, of initiating a new campaign of excavations at Tello (ancient Girsu). What was, therefore, the 21st field season at the site in November of that year marked the launch of a new research and training program, now hosted at the British Museum. Centered on the religious metropolis of Girsu, it consequently signals a new beginning in the search for the origins of the city and its significance in relation to the birth of the state, the invention of cuneiform writing, and the development of complex societies in Ancient Sumer.

I should like first of all to express my gratitude to the Ministry of Tourism and Antiquities of Iraq and the State Board of Antiquities and Heritage for granting me and Fatma Husain a permit to re-explore this truly exceptional site of Iraqi and world heritage. My heartfelt thanks go to Deputy Tourism and Antiquities Minister Mr. Qais Hussein Rashid and Director of Excavations Dr. Haider Abd al-Wahed al-Mamori. Extended thanks go to the authorities in Baghdad, including Mr. Adil Jabour Diwan, Dr. Ahmad Kamel, Mr. Saleem Khalaf Anaeed, and Mr. Hussain Ali Habib, and, in Nasiriya (Thi Qar province), Mr. Amjad Nahma Shabib, SBAH representatives, and Thi Qar archaeological armed forces. Also, I thank Dr. Abdulamir al-Hamdani and Dr. Jaafar Jotheri for their unfailing help and support.

Today, Tello-Girsu is the southern site of the British Museum Iraq Emergency Heritage Management Training Program. I feel particularly fortunate and honored to be part of this venerable institution and, in particular this truly exceptional scheme, and and to work amongst a remarkable staff including the IEHMTP team and the Middle East department. I would like to express my deepest gratitude to Keeper Jonathan Tubb for his powerful encouragement and guidance. I extend my appreciation to St John Simpson, John MacGinnis, Irving Finkel, Sarah Collins, Jonathan Taylor, Alexandra Fletcher, the Ur Project team, and the entire department for their contributions to my inspiration and knowledge and other help in creating this book. It has been made possible by the Museum Scholarly Publications Support Fund, and in this respect, my sincere thanks go to Jeremy Hill and Sarah Faulks for their support. Extended thanks go to David Davison and Rajka Makjanic from Archaeopress Publishing Ltd, and to Simone Rotella who managed to capture in his art my vision of Sumerian sacredness and religious landscapes.

The present book is a compilation of expanded or enhanced papers read over the past few years in various conferences or workshops, most of them prepared in close collaboration with Camille Lecompte to whom, I fear, I have contracted a staggering debt: I acknowledge that debt to him here.

Important contributions to the final form of this book have stemmed from fruitful exchanges with a number of colleagues, including especially the late Tony Wilkinson, Haider al-Mamori, Abdulamir al-Hamdani, Stephanie Rost, and Jaafar Jotheri: to all I offer my warmest thanks.

I am greatly indebted to Julien Chanteau for a number of illuminating comments or suggestions as to how some of the archaeological materials utilized in this book might be more solidly, by which I mean, aesthetically, symbolically, and structurally interpreted.

The Tello-Ancient Girsu project would never have seen the light of day without the wholehearted support of Julien Chanteau and Joyce Nassar, and, above all, the willpower of Fatma Husain to whom my debt of gratitude is unfathomable.

*

As evidenced by the title For the Gods of Girsu: City-State Formation in Ancient Sumer, I acknowledge from the outset that cult played a paramount role in the complex development of the Sumerian city-states. I believe in Arthur Hocart's masterly thesis that kingship and government originated in, and developed from, ritual organization. Critics will argue that I take religion too seriously. I do, because, to paraphrase Aage Westenholz, 'there is ample documentation that the Sumerians also did' (2002, p. 24).

I have envisaged the plan of the book to follow the route of a centrifugal ritual procession in honor of the tutelary god of Girsu: from the Sacred City (Chapter 2), across the Countryside (Chapter 3), to the Border of the city-state (Chapter 4). Chapter 1 corresponds to the *status quaestionis* and a homage to the archaeologist pioneers of Tello. My methodology relies entirely on the combination of various sources of information, and therefore attempts to develop a 'total history' – an approach dear to the heart of the historian Marc Bloch (The Royal Touch).

The Sumerian anthroponyms, theonyms, and toponyms are rendered in Roman characters either in their current transcription (Urukagina, Enki, Nippur, Eanna) or in their component parts ($\tilde{G}ir_2$-su^{ki}, E_2-ninnu). Most vowels and consonants retain their usual value in English. Yet:

— u is always pronounced oo (Uruk = Oorook)
— š denotes sh (Gilgameš = Gilgamesh)
— ḫ corresponds to kh or ch like Loch Ness (Ninḫursag = Ninkhursag)

— g̃ is pronounced ng (sag̃g̃a = sanga)
— all the consonants are articulated (ziqqurrat is pronounced ziqqoorratt)
— and they are voiced, or hard (Ningirsu is pronounced Nin-gir-soo)

Subscript Arabic numerals that accompany certain terms (e_2, bad_3, $ensi_2$) have no phonetic significance and refer to different cuneiform signs. Superscript Roman letters or terms placed before or after other words reflect the use in the cuneiform writing system of determinatives (pre- or post-) which indicate the semantic category to which the words belong: the superscript [d] in ^{d}Enlil is used to indicate that Enlil is the name of a god (^{d} is the abbreviation for dingir, the Sumerian term for deity); the post-determinative [ki] in Lagaš^{ki} indicates that Lagaš is a city.

Introduction: Concept of the Sumerian City-State

For the god Ningirsu, hero of the god Enlil, Urukagina sovereign of Girsu, built in the town of Antasura (Northern[?] Boundary), his E-ḫegal-kalama (House – prosperity of the land); he built the temple of the goddess Ba'u (in Girsu). For the god Igalim he built E-meḫušgal-anki (House of the Great, Fearsome Me of Heaven and Earth), for the god Šulšagana he built his Kituš-akkile (Seat of Lamentations). For the goddess Nanše, he dug her beloved canal, the Niğen-DU-a canal.[1]

The city-state represented the principal form of sociopolitical organization in the Sumerian civilization of the Early Dynastic period (or Presargonic, Protodynastic, ca. 2900-2350 BC), and has therefore long been the focus of scholarly and authoritative studies.[2] Ancient Sumer in Presargonic times appears as a multifaceted or protean mosaic of rival city-states (Ur, Uruk, Girsu-Lagaš, Umma-Zabalam) formed by one or several urban political and religious centers and a countryside composed of a relatively dense network of rural habitats of varying nature. These micro-States of the alluvial plain traversed by an anastomosing river system, striving in particular for the control of large irrigated land areas, were separated by territorial boundaries sanctioned at the magicoreligious level by steles and chapels dedicated to the principal gods of the Sumerian pantheon.

The bipolar territory established like the Greek polis on both urban and rural components belonged, on the basis of the official ideology propounded and transmitted by royal inscriptions, entirely to the gods that the sovereigns, perceived as their earthly representatives or legates, ruled on their order. An, the god of Heaven, founding ancestor of the celestial ruling dynasty, the source and guarantor of total power, resided at Uruk in the Eanna (Temple of Heaven) alongside his hetaera Inanna (Lady of Heaven), the goddess of carnal love and warfare. Enlil (Lord Air), the sovereign god of the cosmos and leading deity of the pantheon, worshiped at Nippur in the Temple of the Mountain (Ekur), presided over the plenary assembly of gods and held as a sign of supreme authority the Tablet of Destinies, a supernatural tablet, emblem and talisman of power. Enki, the water-god, creator of all techniques and expert in magic, ruled at Eridu from the Eabzu (Temple of Apsu, the Watery Deep or Abyss).[3]

---

[1] Cf. Frayne, D. 2008, p. 266-267, URU-KA-gina E1.9.9.2.
[2] Cf. Steinkeller, P. 1993, p. 107-129, Glassner, J.-J. 2000, p. 35-53, Westenholz, A. 2002, p. 23-42 on the Sumerian city-state concept.
[3] Cf. Jacobsen, T. 1976, Kramer, S. N. 1989, Bottéro, J. 2001 (1998) on the Sumerian pantheon. See George, A. 1993 on the Sumerian temples.

Ritual processions carried out repeatedly to commemorate supernatural events through the cities' hinterlands in honor of their tutelary deities, and offerings for rural shrines and boundary sanctuaries, guaranteed a form of religious territorial cohesion.[4] This theological concept of space appears in Presargonic hymns (ca. 2500-2350 BC) in which Enlil apparently assigns cult places to the gods,[5] as well as cosmological accounts of the Old Babylonian period (ca. 2000-1750 BC) which, like the famous myth Enki, the Organization of the Earth and its Cultural Processes, provide comparable mythological motifs.[6] By establishing sanctuaries at Eridu or Ur, only after regaining the supreme knowledge of Enlil and the Me powers of the Ekur temple, Enki organizes the religious axes of the land. The myth transcribes a sacred division of the Sumerian territory between the gods: Enlil at Nippur, Enki at Eridu, and so forth. The 'crafty god' proceeds to organize the entire world in a centripetal system where everything converged on Sumer (Ki'engi) held as the center of the universe:

> Proudly the king stepped forth: Enki the venerable came up to the land. Because the great prince came up to his land, opulence prevailed above and below (everywhere). Enki decrees its fate: 'Sumer, great land, infinite territory, robed in enduring light, settling the Me godly powers upon the people from sunrise to sunset, your Me powers are lofty Me, untouchable, your heart is a maze, unfathomable'.[7]

In Ancient Sumer, the theocentric liturgy revolved entirely around the service to the gods, the 'maintenance of the holders of the sacred'.[8] Protodynastic sovereigns never ceased to pride themselves in their dedicatory or commemorative inscriptions for their zeal in religious behavior and of having undertaken and completed the construction or renovation of magnificent temples to serve as abodes to their poliad demiurges. The divine cult was one of the 'cardinal points and the primary driving force' of the Sumerians,[9] the ruler of course, the 'executor of the rituals' (to speak like Hocart), the clergy or the 'officiants of the rituals' (again Hocart), and the people, all servants and providers of the gods. Rulers furthermore arrogated for themselves the monopoly of edilitarian activities or ex officio obligations related to the organization of the state: the planning of urban space and the countryside, the defense of the land, the supervision of the hydrographic network, the erection of magical or apotropaic border steles.

---

[4] Cf. Selz, G. 1990, p. 111-142; 1995.
[5] Cf. Westenholz, A. 2002, p. 35.
[6] Cf. Kramer, S. N. 1989, p. 38-56.
[7] Cf. Bottéro, J. & Kramer, S. N. 1989, p. 71; Kramer, S. N. 1989, p. 45.
[8] Cf. Bottéro, J. 2001 (1998), p. 114.
[9] Ibid, p. 154.

Prime cities held for being prehistoric centers of cult that crystalized around charismatically imbued proto-urban sanctuaries (perhaps the Ekur of Nippur, certainly the Eanna of Uruk, the Eabzu of Eridu, and in all likelihood the Eninnu of Girsu) were perceived altogether as ceremonial places, managerial -, trade -, and decision-making centers, sheltering the organs of government and the corporations or guilds. At the apex of the city-states' apparatus, the rulers (Sumerian lugal, ensi$_2$) and their household (princely or royal super-houses comparable to the Greek oikos), flanked by a ruling class composed of the clergy (Sumerian sag̃g̃a, gala, archpriests, priests) and notables or vassal dignities to some extent subservient and serving in assemblies of elders, and a cohort of administrators, magistrates, high officials, prebendary superintendents (Sumerian nu-banda$_3$, ugula), managed the property and agrarian domains particularly of the temples, theoretically belonging to the gods, and guaranteed order. In sum a real coexistence of royal and private institutions duly hierarchized perceived as 'gigantic sprawling organizations'[10] composed of urban storehouses, rural granaries, workshops, and large properties or plots of lands.[11]

Despite the political fragmentation of the Sumerian territory, the chief cities formed a sort of amphictyony around the cult of Enlil at Nippur and were at times grouped into volatile pan-Sumerian poliad leagues such as the ephemeral Hexapolis including Šuruppak, Umma, Uruk, Nippur, Adab, and Lagaš,[12] or more viable politico-religious supra-regional entities like Ur-Eridu, Girsu-Lagaš-Nig̃en, or Umma-Zabalam.[13]

*

If such a theoretical or general abstract model of the Sumerian city-state of the Early Dynastic period, for which Girsu-Lagaš has often been regarded as the archetype, appears to be the subject of broad consent among Mesopotamian scholars – with the notable exception of J.-J. Glassner who speculated about the relevance of the concept, rightly recalling that it had been originally created to designate pre-Imperial Rome at the dawn of its territorial expansion –[14] the specifics relating in particular to the spatial organization of these archaic states of varying forms remain to be thoroughly re-examined. A. Westenholz pointed out that although the pseudo-archetype of the Sumerian city-state, Lagaš centered on the official cultic place of Girsu, has been properly estimated by I. Diakonoff to encompass about 3000 square-kilometers of irrigated lands,[15] it may well have been significantly larger than the average.[16]

---

[10] Cf. Forest, J.-D. 1996, p. 207-239.
[11] Cf. Maekawa, K. 1973/74, p. 77-144.
[12] Cf. Pomponio, F. & Visicato, G. 1994.
[13] Cf. Sallaberger, W. & Schrakamp, I. (Ed.) 2015; Lecompte, C. forthcoming.
[14] Cf. Glassner J.-J. 2000, p. 35-53.
[15] Cf. Diakonoff, I. 1956, p. 173-203.
[16] Cf. Westenholz, A. 2002, p. 26.

Seeking to reconstruct archaic syncretism and the development of the Lagaš pantheon from Presargonic offering lists recording the sacrifices distributed to the gods of Girsu and their sanctuaries, G. Selz has elegantly established a strong connection if not a consubstantial relation between the theological credos and the political construct, 'the formation of the pantheon providing a *raison d'être* for the state of Lagaš'.[17] Although Gatumdu was the tutelary goddess of the state's eponymous city of Lagaš (present-day al-Hiba), Ningirsu worshipped in the magnificent Eninnu temple at Girsu (modern Tello) was the principal protector god (and the 'nucleus of the Lagaš pantheon') that exercised lordship over the entire Early Dynastic city-state, which also included Niĝen/Nina (present-day Zurghul), the center of Nanše cult. Hence the Lagaš First Dynasty (hereafter Lagaš I) state included, perhaps since Ur-Nanše, the founder of the dynasty originating from Gur-sar, a triad of first-tier centers and sanctuaries, but also important rural cult-places and nonurban religious complexes. Girsu including its sanctum sanctorum (Uruku), considered to be the primary seat of the tutelary deity, was the sacred metropolis and central pole of the city-state.

That the rulers from Ur-Nanše to Urukagina generally took the title of 'ensi$_2$- or rarely lugal-Lagaš^{ki}' instead of -Gir$_2$-su^{ki} – except for Urukagina, but that was only after having lost the city of Lagaš to Lugal-zagesi of Umma, so this would appear to be self-explanatory – has been convincingly explained because Lagaš was probably the archaic political center of a protohistoric state.[18] Another nonexclusive reason may be related to the apparent pious character or connotation of the title ensi$_2$, the literal meaning of which remains obscure and whose roots appear to be set deeply in the darkness of prehistoric times, yet clearly denoting a tremendous deference or reverence to a supernatural overlord. Presargonic rulers of the city-state of Girsu-Lagaš probably believed that the true liege of Girsu was their patron god (literally 'Lord of Girsu'), hence preferring the titulature of legate and sovereign of Lagaš.

To be sure Early Dynastic Girsu-Lagaš should hardly be held as the archetypal model of the Sumerian city-state which can only be abstracted and referred to as an operative or heuristic concept – a hybrid form of sociopolitical organization in Ancient Sumer. Yet because of the truly exceptional richness of information from Tello produced since the heroic age of the Mesopotamian archaeologist pioneers – the large-scale religious and secular architecture, royal statuary, and cuneiform tablets – Presargonic Girsu clearly stands out as a prime locus for re-analyzing, by means of an interdisciplinary approach combining archaeology, epigraphy, and space imagery, its topographical layout and regional setting in order to offer new insights into the institutional form and territorial organization of an Early Dynastic Sumerian city-state.

---

[17] Cf. Selz, G. 1990, p. 111-142, 1995.
[18] Ibid, p. 118.

Chapter One

Once Upon a Time in Ancient Girsu. Or Tello and the Rediscovery of the Sumerians

Tello truly is a land of wonders! For 20 years I have been relentlessly exploring the site, never has there been a day without a brilliant find to crown such tremendous labors. And once again statues, steles, tablets compensate me for my drudgery. But the masterpiece is a copper blade from the time of Ur-Nanše.

Ernest de Sarzec, Iraq, 1898

Tello/Girsu and the Sumerian Miracle

The archaeological site of Tello, the modern Arabic toponym of ancient Girsu – sanctuary of the heroic deity Ningirsu resurrected only thanks to the fierce desire and determination of the last archaeologist-consul of Mesopotamia, Ernest de Sarzec (1832-1901) who paid for it with his life – brought to the scientific world the revelation of the Sumerians.

Of course Ancient Mesopotamia, the 'Land between rivers' (the Tigris and the Euphrates), had not completely fallen into oblivion. But before the excavations of Assyrian palaces of Sargon II and Ashurbanipal from 1843 and the discovery of the royal inscriptions of Girsu and the sacerdotal library of Nippur at the end of the 19th century our knowledge of the Fertile Crescent remained limited (a few names of legendary places, Mesopotamian kings and gods, mythical heroes), and our sources on the Cradle of Civilization scarce (the Bible, Classical authors, Arabic and Persian scholars, travelers' tales).[19] Babylon and the Garden of Eden have inspired since the Early Renaissance the Arts and Humanities.

Bruegel the Elder (1525-1569) painted the Tower of Babel symbolizing the vanity and transience of earthly efforts (Fig. 1); Blake (1757-1827) portrayed the bestial madness of Nebuchadnezzar, the avatar of oriental despotism and pagan hubris, and Delacroix (1798-1863) painted the Death of Sardanapalus, a metaphor of voluntary servitude. This completely fantasized (or phantasmal) and relatively recent past of Mesopotamia – because contemporaneous with the Bible and Assyrian-Babylonian monarchs – truly fascinated as much as it horrified Europe. But the reminiscences of the earliest times of Sumer concomitant with the rise of the state, the creation of cuneiform writing, the emergence of an archaic 'world-system', the development of

---

[19] Cf. Lion, B. & Michel, C. 2009, p. 15-32.

Fig. 1: The Tower of Babel by Bruegel the Elder
(Museum Boijmans Van Beuningen of Rotterdam).

the arts and craft (sculpture, cylinder seals, monumental architecture), in short, the principal components of the 'Sumerian Miracle', had been totally forgotten.

Archaeological research in Mesopotamia really started in 1843, approximatively 50 years after Bonaparte's Egyptian campaign that inaugurated, to be sure at the point of the bayonet, Scientific Orientalism. Yet if the resounding discoveries of Consul Paul-Émile Botta (1802-1870) at Khorsabad (Dūr-Šarrukīn), including reliefs and royal inscriptions of Sargon II, followed by the truly spectacular excavations of Sir Henry Layard (1817-1894) first at Nimrud (ancient Kalhu), which yielded bas-reliefs and human-headed winged bulls from the palace of Ashurnasirpal II, then at Nineveh (present-day Kuyunjik), which uncovered the capital of Sennacherib and the Royal Library of Ashurbanipal destroyed in 612 BC by the Medes and Babylonians, took place in Assyria, the Land of Sumer, dreaded then both for its harsh environment and warring tribes had been almost completely forsaken by the first explorers. The landing of the vice-consul Ernest de Sarzec in Basra in 1877 (from the Red Sea) and the first explorations of Tello – prelude to the reappearance of the Sumerians – represent therefore a milestone of these pioneering researches.

According to the philologist Jules Oppert (1825-1905), it was the most significant discovery in Mesopotamia after those of Nineveh and Babylon.[20]

It was probably during the reign of Emperor Napoléon III that the future discoverer of Tello, Ernest Chocquin, then gas director of the Company Lebon in Alexandria (Egypt), registered as civil engineer from 1864 to 1868 (according to a note of the Foreign Affairs), adopted the patronymic or alias de Sarzec. In the aftermath of the French collapse of 1870 against Prussia a decree of 1872 appointed him consular officer of the French Republic to Massawa (Eritrea) in one of the African provinces of the Sublime Porte. But in these Abyssinian marches, Ernest de Sarzec stayed just four years, only to witness the failure of the expansionist attempts of Ismaïl Pacha, Khedive (viceroy) of Egypt against the Ethiopian state of the Negus (king of kings) Yohannes IV. In 1875 under the presidency of MacMahon the explorer-diplomat received from Metropole his assignment to Basra. That he already fostered a passion for archaeology even before his departure for the floodplain of Southern Iraq is proven by archival consular and political correspondences wherein he reported, e.g. in 1875, ancient and forgotten ruins 'in the kind of Gondar and Axum'. One may still contemplate (he wrote) fine remnants of Greek temples (in fact probably dating from the Aksumite empire) as well as well-preserved remains of a splendid palace of Greek style, once the residence of great kings.[21]

In Mesopotamia, after the first gropings and peregrinations of the explorers of the East India Company in post in Baghdad carried out at the twilight of the Enlightenment, the *coups d'éclat* of both Botta and Layard in the heartland of the Assyrian Empire from 1850 heralded the great discoveries of the late 19th century and the time of the Mandates: Nippur, Ur, Uruk, Babylon, Assur, Mari. In this particularly auspicious context, the first excavations at Tello in 1877 by the former consul-explorer of the high Abyssinian plateaus, were nevertheless singular because they led precisely to the discovery of the thriving pristine and then completely forgotten Sumerian civilization.

Despite the official account somewhat romanticized or idealized in the classic work Discoveries in Chaldea giving pride of place to Ernest de Sarzec's findings and reconnaissance, in particular the discovery in 1877 of a 'magnificent colossal statue' of the ruler Gudea, it appears rather clear that the early archaic statuary from Tello had been in fact already unearthed before the arrival of the vice-consul in Basra.[22] The fact remains that the powerful insight and perspicacity of Ernest de Sarzec led him to recognize the incomparable value of the recently exhumed artefacts, and to further explore the site, first from his personal funds, then at the expense of the French Republic (Fig. 2 & 3).

---

[20] Cf. Pillet, M. 1958, p. 52-66.
[21] Ibid, p. 52-66.
[22] Cf. Parrot, A. 1948, p. 14-33.

FIG. 2: ERNEST DE SARZEC AND HIS ESCORT AT TELLO
(SARZEC, E. & HEUZEY, L. 1884-1912, PL. 63-2).

FIG. 3: APOTROPAIC PILLAR COMPOSED OF INSCRIBED BRICKS FROM GUDEA
(SARZEC, E. & HEUZEY, L. 1884-1912, PL. 52-2).

Once Upon a Time in Ancient Girsu. Or Tello and the Rediscovery of the Sumerians

And the harvest of Sumerian antiques proved to be truly abundant: inscribed statues, cuneiform tablets, foundation deposits, alabaster reliefs. Such spectacular finds almost immediately warranted the support of the first curator of the Department of Oriental Antiquities, Léon Heuzey (1831-1922) who, from the Louvre, bestowed Ernest de Sarzec guidance becoming something of a 'deus ex machina' of Tello.[23]

In Babylonia the general conditions remained however difficult and the field-work conducted by the consul often interrupted due to logistical problems and endemic violence in the region, including the revolt of the powerful Muntafiq confederacy of Arab tribes against the Ottoman Empire. Ernest de Sarzec effected his last excavations at Tello in 1900. Yet some of the artefacts unearthed during the eleven campaigns in the Seleucid palace of the potentate Adad-nadin-aḫḫe (mainly the statuary of Gudea) and especially in the Eninnu temple (the Presargonic sanctuary of the patron-god Ningirsu) already counted among the masterpieces of the Sumerian civilization: the Stele of the Vultures (or victory stele of E-anatum of Lagaš), probably the earliest-known historiographical document relating the recurring conflict between the Early Dynastic city-states of Girsu-Lagaš and Umma-Zabalam (Fig. 4); the well-known liturgical silver vase of En-metena dedicated to Ningirsu; the alabaster votive relief of Ur-Nanše representing Imdugud (or Anzu) as a lion-headed eagle, the demigod tempest-bird and protector of Girsu, emblem of Ningirsu; the Ur-Nanše bas-relief celebrating the religious deed of the founder of the first dynasty of Lagaš presiding

Fig. 4: Stele of the Vultures. Mythological side depicting the heroic war-god Ningirsu and the tempest-bird Imdugud (Sarzec, E. & Heuzey, L. 1884-1912, pl. 4-bis).

---

[23] Cf. Pillet, M. 1958, p. 52-66.

over the rituals of (re)foundation of the state's principal sanctuary; and of course the Gudea cylinders recounting the mythical construction of the Eninnu sanctum sanctorum and the enthronement of Ningirsu and Ba'u, the chief-god's consort.

Ernest de Sarzec was succeeded by Gaston Cros (1861-1915), a French army commander who as head of the expedition to Chaldea led four excavation campaigns at Tello between 1901 and 1909. Great connoisseur of desolate landscapes, the officer from Saint-Cyr, previously attached to the Army Geographic Service from 1891 to 1893, had developed a thorough understanding of desert topography by carrying out several topographical surveys of the Sahara. Besides the renewed discovery of statues, fragments of stelae, clay tablets, and other significant artefacts, some dating from the earliest periods of the Sumerian civilization, the captain (promoted to chief battalion in 1905), clearly more vigilant to mud-brick remnants than his predecessor, may well have boasted legitimately of having exposed the truly exceptional 10 meter-wide Gudea temenos-enceinte featuring terracotta magical inscribed cones (Fig. 5).

Gaston Cros was also one of the first explorers to conduct systematically 'scientific reconnaissance' of the site's environs and investigate its geographical setting. The pioneering prospections performed on horseback from 1903 represent the forerunners of the 1960-1970 emblematic regional surveys (The Uruk Countryside, Heartland of Cities) led by R. Adams and H. Nissen, or by T. Jacobsen, that deeply reevaluated inter alia the conceptual model of the Hydraulic State theorized by Karl Wittfogel (Oriental Despotism). The classic monograph New Excavations at Tello published in 1911 received praise from academia, welcomed by the British Royal Asiatic Society 'as one of the most important on the subject of ancient Sumeria'.[24]

Sadly Gaston Cros had to leave the Mesopotamian delta in 1909 never to return again. Promoted to lieutenant-colonel in 1912, he was transferred to a regiment in Africa and participated in the French expedition against the Zaian confederation of Berber tribes led by Hubert Lyautey, Resident General of the French protectorate in Morocco. After the outbreak of the Great War Gaston Cros returned to metropolitan France and fought in defense of Paris at the First Battle of the Marne, then, promoted to colonel, received command of the Moroccan brigade on the Yser composed ad hoc of tirailleurs and zouaves. He fell on the field of battle on the front of Artois in 1915. Shortly before his death, in the Flanders' trenches, he wrote to Léon Heuzey these words imbued with irony (and wit) but not deprived of tragedy: 'I am still at heart an archaeologist. As in the glorious days of Tello, I carry out formidable earthworks; yet instead of Gudea cones, I find German shells: this also does not lack interest!'.[25]

---

[24] Cf. Pinches, T.G. 1912, p. 829–831.
[25] Cf. Heuzey, L. 1915, p. 244-245.

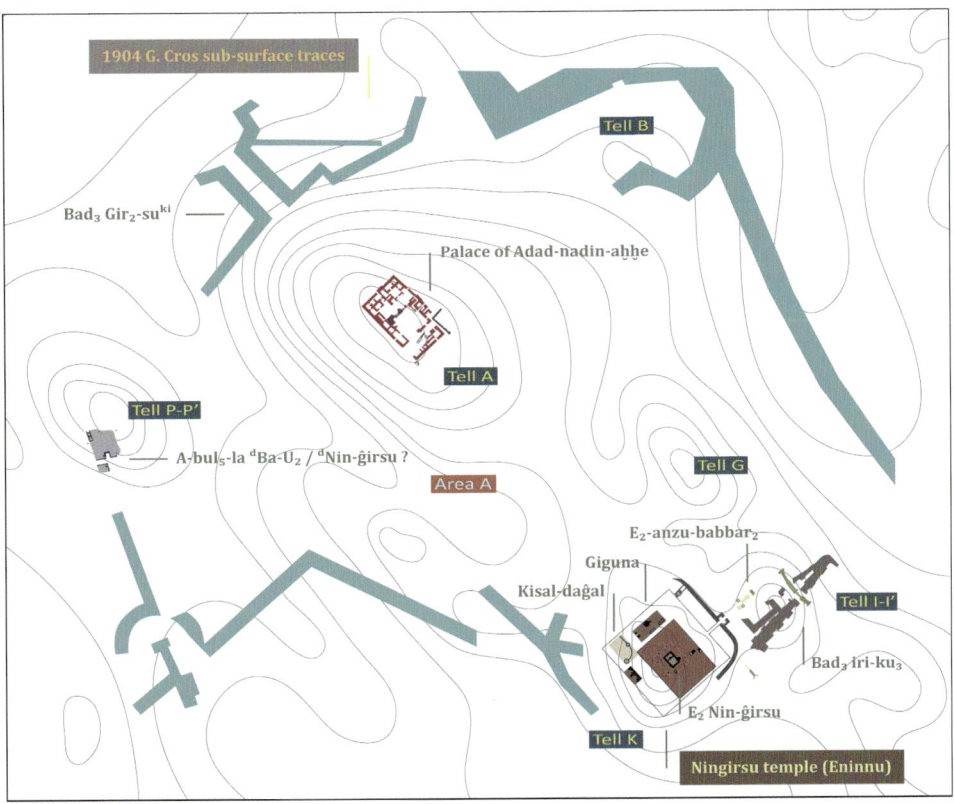

FIG. 5: SPATIAL ORGANIZATION OF THE SACRED PRECINCT OF GIRSU RECONSTRUCTED BY COMPILING AND GEO-RECTIFYING THE OLD PLANS PRODUCED BY E. DE SARZEC AND G. CROS, SUCH AS THE FIRST CONTOUR MAP COMPLETED BETWEEN 1888 AND 1893, THE PRINCIPAL EXPOSED ARCHITECTURAL RUINS INCLUDING THE TEMPLE OF NINGIRSU (ENINNU), THE GUDEA TEMENOS-WALL, AND THE 1904 SUB-SURFACE NETWORK OF FORTIFICATIONS.

After a break of twenty years in the course of which Tello was regularly looted producing statues of Gudea and Ur-Ningirsu, cuneiform tablets, Henri de Genouillac (1881-1940) resumed the site exploration in 1929 until 1931. Specialist of the epigraphical material from Tello, he had previously supervised in Babylonia in 1912 excavations at the important Agadean site of Kiš in the ancient heartland of Sargon's Empire, and where according to the well-known semi-mythical Sumerian King List 'kingship had descended from heaven after the flood had swept away Mesopotamia'. Henri de Genouillac carried out three campaigns at Tello before entrusting the expedition from 1932 to 1933 to André Parrot (1901-1980), the future inventor of Mari on the Euphrates, the mythical postdiluvian 10th dynasty to hold kingship over Mesopotamia. Among the latest most significant Sumerian finds unearthed at Tello during the regular excavations that came to an end in 1933 was a headed bull statuette dedicated to

Urgar bearing the four-tier horned tiara, in all likelihood according to André Parrot 'the prototype of Assyrian giant bulls from Khorsabad and Nimrud'.[26]

Overall, twenty planned archaeological campaigns took place in ancient Girsu between 1877 and 1933 conducted by four leading figures pursuing atypical paths alternately legate, warrior, priest, and curator, yet all driven by the same passion for the Sumerians. That the large-scale excavations of Tello were, however, to the very least approximate is certain. They were pioneering and therefore carried out by methods that clearly bear the ineffaceable mark of their era – the Industrial Revolution both in the techniques and logistics – that prove indeed catastrophic by present standards. Nevertheless: the legacy of the first explorers of Chaldea appears truly colossal.

The Myth of the Archaic Temple-City

It was indeed from the myriads of Presargonic cuneiform tablets of Girsu that was developed in the aftermath of World War I by the theologian A. Deimel the famous theory of the Sumerian temple-city (or temple-state) subsequently revised by A. Falkenstein.[27] A redistributive system of the Sumerian archaic state perceived as a primitive theocracy (or ecclesiastical lordship) where the authority was first held by a priest-king serving the principal temple of the patron deity, the sole proprietor of the large agricultural domains, and thus the only entity able to produce surplus. Yet this theocratic order would have been supplanted in the course of the 3rd Millennium by a secular political power (or royal) relying on a complex palatial-type administrative bureaucracy.

The famous Reform texts of Urukagina, the last ruler of the first dynasty of Lagaš (at the time of Lugal-zagesi of Umma and Sargon of Akkad), inscribed on exceptional clay cones discovered by E. de Sarzec at Tello, would have precisely illustrated the development of a royal power separated from priesthood and the temple establishment, personified by a lugal (or 'great man').[28] This change was connected with a formulation where it is stated:

> He (URA-KA-gina) installed the god Ningirsu (city god of Girsu) as proprietor over the ruler's estate and the king's fields; he installed the goddess Ba'u (Ningirsu's consort) as proprietor of the estate of the woman's organization and the fields of the woman's establishment; and he installed the god Šulšagana as proprietor of the children's estate.[29]

---

[26] Cf. Parrot, A. 1948, p. 146-147.
[27] Cf. Deimel, A. 1931; Falkenstein, A. 1974.
[28] Cf. Glassner, J.-J. 2000, p. 35-53.
[29] Cf. Frayne, D. 2008, p. 262, URA-KA-gina E1.9.9.1.

As pointed out by H. Nissen this classic passage was generally interpreted as meaning that the economic units and estates in question had in the past belonged to the gods, were then usurped by the ruler and his family, and were now being returned to their original owners (Girsu's pantheon) by the devout prince Urukagina in an attempt to restore the old order and protect the people from officials' abuse.[30]

Yet based on elements obviously too speculative, the Sumerian temple-city model was criticized, first in 1950-1960 by the linguists I. Diakonoff and I. Gelb who proved by a systematic review of Girsu Early Dynastic archives the existence of private property within the economy of the city-state,[31] then in 1970-1980 by the philologists K. Maekawa and B. Foster who established the singularity of the reforms of Urukagina, probably an usurper seeking to return the landed property and estate of the city-state that had been gradually appropriated by his predecessors back under the aegis of the principal gods of the pantheon of Girsu.[32] Hence it seems more likely that the ruler's gesture, far from being a historical paradigm, may have been on the contrary an epiphenomenon circumscribed to Girsu.

Primitive Democracy or Polyarchy?

It is probably not completely trivial if the famous counter-theory of the Urukian primitive democracy formulated by the Sumerologist T. Jacobsen was released in 1943 after almost all of Europe fell into the sphere of influence of the totalitarian state of the Third Reich.[33] Based primarily on the frequent logograms reflecting a sort of proto-assembly (UNKIN) in the epic of Gilgameš and Akka and the myth of Lugal-e (or the genesis of kingship), it brought a very different view of the protohistory of Mesopotamia emphasizing the existence in the Late Uruk period (ca. 3200-3000 BC) of a democratic-kind political system – thus the antithesis of the conceptual model of the archaic temple-city – which would have been gradually supplanted in the course of the 3rd Millennium by a form of autocratic power.

Though both theories are so fundamentally opposing as to the origins or nature of political regimes and the sources of power at the dawn of history, they nevertheless concur as to the sequence of the development and the modalities of the evolution of power throughout the Early Dynastic period culminating in the rise of kingship. Monuments of Presargonic–Lagaš II art such as the Stele of Vultures or the Plaque of Ur-Nanše were interpreted as clear embodiments of a new political system characterizing the Classical Sumerian city-state.

---

[30] Cf. Nissen, H. 1990, p. 147.
[31] Cf. Diakonoff, I. 1974; Gelb, I. 1969, p. 137-154.
[32] Cf. Maekawa, K. 1973/74, p. 77-144; Foster, B. 1981, p. 225-241.
[33] Cf. Jacobsen, T. 1943, p. 159-172.

The hypothesis of an archaic council depositary of the political power in Ancient Sumer was enhanced in 1990-2000 by G. Selz and especially J.-J. Glassner who argued its existence not only on the basis of mythological and epic works of the Ur III period and the time of Hammurabi of Babylon (ca. 2100-1800 BC) but on the basis of lexicographical tablets of the Late Uruk period.[34] Although G. Selz suggested that the archaic assembly may have restricted the central government of nascent states, J.-J. Glassner rejected the idea of primitive authority completely devoted to a priest-king advocating for a system of co-leadership of power among dignitaries of equal ranks. If the relevance of the Sumerian priest-king concept involving a unity of the political and religious spheres at the origins of the State often utilized by Mesopotamian scholars to define the archetypal form of power in Late Uruk times appears highly equivocal – the priest-king being the 'greatest cumulator of all, the source of all powers' to borrow Hocart's phraseology – the aforementioned argument that the first State would have been characterized by a relatively democratic political system, or polyarchical,[35] remains however to be thoroughly demonstrated.

Yet that the primitive assembly composed of notables of rather equivalent ranks provided with attributes or insignia, probably noticeable in the Urukian glyptic and figurative art, had been overpowered during the Early Dynastic period by an autocratic regime seems in fact established on the basis of inscribed votive artefacts from Girsu and in light of the Royal tombs of Ur and especially their accompanying dead, concept dear to the heart of the anthropologist A. Testart (Voluntary Servitude). Overall, though concepts like theocratic polity, primitive democracy, or polyarchical regime certainly possess important heuristic or epistemological interest, they tend to become rather controversial whenever they are employed as exclusive explanatory models.

Standing in the Shadows of Giants

Today, after 130 years of research first led by the pioneers of Sumerian archeology (E. de Sarzec, G. Cros) and the decipherers and creators of Sumerology (J. Oppert, F. Thureau-Dangin) amplified by visionary researchers (S. N. Kramer, T. Jacobsen, R. McC. Adams), and thanks to the availability of recently declassified Cold War space imagery and especially the possibility to launch new explorations in Southern Iraq, it seems important to perpetuate, and even in some respects to renew this Herculean work in particular on the subject of early state formation in Mesopotamia. New agendas of authoritative scholars like P. Steinkeller on the city–countryside relationship and the importance of rural networks in Ur III times, or G. Selz on the gods, pilgrimage rituals, and religious festivals in the Early Dynastic period, have already paved the way forward.

---

[34] Cf. Selz, G. 1998, p. 281-234; Glassner, J.-J. 2000, p. 35-53.
[35] Cf. Glassner, J.-J. 2000, p. 49.

Chapter Two

The City of the Heroic God. The General Layout of a Sumerian Metropolis

E-anatum, ruler of Lagaš, nominated by the god Enlil, granted strength by the god Ningirsu, chosen in the heart by the goddess Nanše, nourished with wholesome milk by the goddess Ninḫursag, given a pleasant name by the goddess Inanna, granted wisdom by the god Enki, restored Girsu for the god Ningirsu, (and) built the wall of the sacred precinct for him.[36]

A Landscape of Spoils as a Legacy of the Pioneers

The French expeditions to Tello/Girsu conducted between 1877 and 1933 led to the identification of a palimpsest of five main periods of occupation, including the protohistorical times (Ubaid, Uruk, and Jemdat Nasr), the Early Dynastic period (roughly corresponding to the time of the First dynasty of Lagaš), the Akkadian–Ur III periods (including the Second dynasty of Lagaš), the Isin-Larsa–Old Babylonian times, and the Seleucid period (palace of Adad-nadin-aḫḫe). Remains of the Early Dynastic period have been uncovered principally in the central part of the site – that is, at Tell K, also referred to since E. de Sarzec and L. Heuzey as the mound of the *Maison des fruits*, the sole stratigraphic sequence of Lagaš I temple structures, Tell I (Tell I'), Tell P (Tell P') the so-called *Porte du Diable* after G. Cros – and probably at the Eastern tells under H. de Genouillac and A. Parrot. Other areas of the site (Tell G, Tell L) also yielded, though scanty, remnants of Protodynastic times.

Most of the Presargonic cuneiform tablets, ca. 1800 tablets and fragments from the queen's agro-managerial household (at the time of En-entarzi, Lugal-Anda, Urukagina), successively called e_2-mi_2, the 'wife's house' and e_2-^{d}Ba-U_2, the temple of the goddess Ba'u (or Baba, Bawu), the divine counterpart to the ruler's wife, were unearthed during non-regular excavations and lootings probably at Tell V, known also as the Mound of the Tablets. By contrast, most of the royal inscriptions have been discovered in the Eninnu temple of Girsu and the Bagara temple of Lagaš (modern al-Hiba). Also, Tello appears to have been heavily plundered between 1909 and 1929, and lootings occurred probably after 1933, as well as in 2003 after the American-led invasion of Iraq. The topographical layout of ancient Girsu has therefore considerably changed over the past 140 years, since the first exploration by E. de Sarzec in 1877. Massive amounts of excavation spoil completely conceal, at least for the central mounds of the site, any significant landscape features of the archaic sacred city (Fig. 6).

---

[36] Cf. Frayne, D. 2008, p. 146-147, E-anatum E1.9.3.5.

Fig. 6: The central complex of mounds of Tello (Tell K, Tell I-I') featuring giant heaps of spoils, archaeological pits, and large ravines, and in the background the Eastern tells (November 2015).

Today the site appears as a complex of mounds rising some 15 meters above the flat alluvial surrounding lands situated on exposed surfaces of a Holocene oval-shaped 'turtleback' measuring ca. 3000 meters in length (from North to South), and 2000 meters in width (from East to West). Only two comprehensive topographic maps were made of the latter including the archaeological mounds: the first accurate plan of the site, including one meter interval contour lines, was carried out between 1888 and 1893 by H. de Sevelinges, the topographer of E. de Sarzec;[37] the second map, yet not correctly oriented – that is, roughly facing North-East – of the whole complex, including the approximately situated excavated areas of previous campaigns, was completed in 1929–31 under the direction of H. de Genouillac.[38] Also, the 1934 publication of the latter features a Royal Air Force un-dated, un-scaled and not geo-rectified aerial photography of the site. Although the plan published in 1948 by A. Parrot is properly oriented – that is, facing North – comprises an increased number of contour lines, and includes the entire field operations conducted since E. de Sarzec, a doubt arises about the fact that the site was re-surveyed between 1931 and

---

[37] Cf. Sarzec, E. de & Heuzey, L. 1884-1912, plan B.
[38] Cf. Genouillac, H. de 1934-36, pl. xiv.

1933 by means of leveling-type instruments: the plan appears to have been merely re-drawn from the previous one.[39] As for the topographic-kind map made by G. Cros in 1903–9 of the large-scale tells of the site, it displays very rough contour lines that do not correspond to the general topography, and major scale errors, including flagrant mis-locations of exposed architectural structures, and therefore seems more likely to have been sketched rather than completed using automatic levels.[40]

Moving Landscapes and the Power of Space Imagery

If the graphic information of Tello in its entirety remains problematic, including of course the detailed plans of Early Dynastic architectonic features – and this fact leading recently Mesopotamian scholars to alter somewhat arbitrary these plans, or even to completely relocate entire field operations, solely on the grounds that pre-Sargonic structures have been so inadequately recorded –[41] the recent availability of declassified space photography offer new and valuable material for archaeological and epigraphic studies of the city's ancient landscape and hinterland.[42] Code-named Corona satellite images taken for the Central Intelligence Agency from 1959 to 1972 have indeed proven to be an important resource not only for the identification of archeological sites on a regional scale but also of previously non-documented tenuous relict surface features. Geo-referenced (i.e., transformed into a geographic co-ordinate system), these images, moreover, permit, from photographic interpretation of specific recurrent landmarks, to ortho-rectify the British air services' imagery and to quasi-geographically correct the topographic maps, that is, to re-project them to a common scale and orientation (Fig. 7). It is therefore possible to reconstruct, through the analysis of these relatively high-resolution photographs, by means of remote-sensing techniques in light of evidence from archaeological and epigraphic studies enhanced by recent ground-control surveys, a new topographic plan of Presargonic Girsu.[43]

The geo-corrected American Corona imagery displaying the 1968 topographical layout of Tello enables first to measure accurately its surface – that is, ca. 130 hectares – an area which is considerably reduced compared to the extremely varying estimates given previously by the French archaeologists who described the site rather impressionistically as having substantially the shape of an oval measuring in length between 3000 and 4000 meters, and in width between 1500 and 3000 meters.[44] Of

---

[39] Cf. Parrot, A. 1948, p. 29.
[40] Cf. Cros, G. 1910, plan K.
[41] Cf. Margueron, J.-C. 2005, p. 63-92; Marchesi, G. & Marchetti, N. 2011, p. 38-44.
[42] Cf. Pournelle, J. 2007, p. 29-62.
[43] Cf. Rey, S. & Lecompte, C. in press.
[44] Cf. Cros, G. 1910, p. 5; Genouillac, H. de 1936, p. 2; Parrot, A. 1948, p. 9. The size of ca. 130 hectares corresponding to the circumvallated space and the so-called western mounds in fact exclude any hypothetical peripheral and suburban areas that existed in the Early Dynastic period. According to the pre-Sargonic administrative documents, Girsu's near periphery included e.g. a nonurban settlement, probably a large village designed as e_2-za$_3$-iri-ka, that is, the 'House (i.e., a village) on the border of the city (of Girsu)', consisting of important rural storage structures

FIG. 7: SUPERIMPOSED 1968 CORONA SPACE PHOTOGRAPHY OF TELLO
(A), GEOGRAPHICALLY CORRECTED PLAN OF 1888-1893 (B), AND ORTHO-RECTIFIED RAF AERIAL IMAGERY (C).

course, the significant difference in assessment of the site's size is largely due to confusion between the proper boundaries of the complex of archeological mounds and the fluctuating delimitations of the elevated 'turtleback' (i.e., Holocene knoll-type geomorphologic feature) upon which the former rests. Also, this could probably account for the fact that the perimeters indicated on the E. de Sarzec plan coincide neither with those of the H. de Genouillac and A. Parrot maps and sketches, nor with those that are perceptible both on the RAF and Corona photographs. If the surface of the 'turtleback' constantly evolved from 1877 to 1968 (and to the present-day), the analysis of the post-World War I aerial photography and the 1968 space imagery reveals evidence of archaic fortification features of probable Early Dynastic date that encompass roughly one-third of its land area.[45]

Even though most of the data produced since E. de Sarzec and L. Heuzey should be subject to caution, the early descriptions of the site's topography by these pioneering Orientalists, as much as the first plan made by H. de Sevelinges and

---

nearby the city (or adjacent to Tello) where e.g. quantity of timber material and reeds were stored (cf. Chapter 3). The Corona space imagery principally used in the present book was taken May 4, 1968 (DS 1103-1041DA057).
[45] Cf. Pournelle, J. 2003, p. 179.

the schematic plan of G. Cros, have proven to be tremendously valuable since, as already mentioned, large heaps of earth littered with broken pottery conceal the topographical features that could have been noticeable either on the RAF imagery or the 1968 Corona photography. Thus, prior to the first large-scale French excavations in the late nineteenth-century Ottoman-era Iraq the site would have appeared as a multi-mounded complex, including two main and unequal precincts of respectively ca. 115 and 15 hectares separated by two major wadi-like gullies running from Northwest to Southeast in opposite directions from a central pass-like feature that clearly stood out in the topography. Both areas comprised many mounds of varying sizes and morphologic types: the spatial organization of the larger district consisted of a northern part of ca. 35 hectares including four first-tier tells ranging from 12 to 14 meters above the surrounding Holocene plains (from North to South: Tell A, Tell K, Tell U, and Tell V), and a relatively flat and homogenous southern part of ca. 80 hectares; the general layout of the eastern district consisted of a series of second- or third-tier tells ranging from 7 to 9 meters in altitude and in alignment from Northwest to Southeast.

Excavations from 1877 to 1933 have produced only unequivocal monumental and elite-related data for the Presargonic period, and therefore no substantial information is available on the non-elite and secular domestic-like sectors of the urban layout.[46] Also, subjected to systematic surface analysis as early as 1904, the site yielded plausible Early Dynastic sub-surface traces of fortification and hydraulic features, including the quasi-complete network of complex mud-brick enceintes featuring firing platforms and defended gates circumvallating part of the main cultic hub of the city (i.e., part of the northern district encompassing Tell A, Tell K and Tell I-I'), and the city-harbor and associated canals (i.e., situated nearby Tell B).[47] Superimposed RAF and Corona imagery made it possible to confirm the identification of some of these linear soil marks that are characteristic either of archaic enceintes or paleo-canals and appear therefore both on the ground and aerial–satellite photography.[48] Careful re-examination of these evanescent and fairly controversial landscape marks that have been mapped by means of remote-sensing methods and confirmed in 2015 by thorough site reconnaissance, and with reference to the archaeological and epigraphic evidence, led to a re-appraisal of the general layout of Protodynastic Girsu (Fig. 8).

The April and November 2015 ground prospections also led to the identification of the previous excavations carried out by the French teams before World War II, including the ruins of the so-called Enigmatic construction (Eastern tells), and the dig house built by H. de Genouillac in 1929, and several important surface

---

[46] Cf. Parrot, A. 1948, p. 54-132.
[47] Cf. Cros, G. 1910, p. 64.
[48] Contra Genouillac, H. de 1936, p. 3, and Parrot, A. 1948, p. 148, who have, therefore, erroneously contradicted the preliminary interpretations of G. Cros.

FIG. 8: PRINCIPAL TOPOGRAPHICAL FEATURES AND QUARTERS OF ANCIENT GIRSU REVEALED BY THE 1968 CORONA SATELLITE IMAGERY, INCLUDING THE SACRED-CITY IRI-KU$_3$ (A), THE CENTRAL AND SOUTHERN AREAS (B), THE EASTERN EXTRAMURAL DISTRICT (C), THE PERIPHERAL TELLS AND SUBURBAN AREAS (D), THE PROBABLE CITY-HARBOR KAR-MA$_2$-ADDIR$_x$ (E), AND THE MEGA-CANAL I$_7$-NIĜEN$_6^{KI}$-DU-A (F).

inscribed objects corresponding to royal inscriptions mostly of Gudea referring to the construction of the well-known Anzu-babbar and others such as the e$_2$-PA e$_2$-ub-imin-a-ni (a rather enigmatic heptagon temple), but also of Ur-Ningirsu II, Ur-Namma, and perhaps two of the Presargonic period including an alabaster fragment of a votive artefact dedicated to the goddess Ba'u.[49]

Multivallation for the Purpose of Coercion and Defense

Overall, no less than two connecting fortification systems have been reconstructed from a multidisciplinary approach: the inner perimeter of ca. 1500 meters already partly identified by G. Cros and enclosing a sacred precinct of certainly large-scale cultic architecture, and a second outer defense perhaps fronted by ditches of ca. 3500 meters detectable both on the RAF and Corona images and probably surrounding a proper urban-type space of combined pre-planned political-religious hubs (i.e., Tell

---

[49] Cf. Rey, S., Husain, F. & Lecompte, C. forthcoming.

V, Tell U, and Tell L) and hypothetical plebeian and secular densely built-up domestic areas (i.e., the most part of the southern flat area of the site). Surveying thoroughly the western lower city in both Spring and Fall of 2015 led to confirm the residential nature of this large-scale space composed of household quarters including large quantity of domestic-type surface artefacts, such as pottery, in addition to hearths, tannour-like ovens, and grinding stones, indicating that, for the most part, activities within the whole area were predominantly domestic in nature, related to the storage, preparation and consumption of food.

Heavy rains revealed in November 2015 subsurface traces of the exterior fortifications at the Southwestern edge of the site. Detectable over a length of about 60 meters, the mud-brick enceinte of approximately 5 meters in width included perhaps an outer-wall some 20 meters apart, 3 or 4 meters in width, and at the intersection of a ravine running perpendicularly to it, creating a break in this otherwise continuous feature, a tower of ca. 6 m by 8 m, probably part of a defended gate. Evidently, if the newly identified fortifications are extremely difficult or impossible to date until renewed excavations, a few uncovered stretches of the inner curtain made of plano-convex mud-bricks and pierced by a defended gate (Tell P-P') have ascertained that at least part of the interior fortifications dates to the Early Dynastic period.[50] In fact, apart from some cuneiform sources, the sole archaeological evidence pertaining to a chronological synchronism between both defensive systems appears to be a stretch of archaic mud-brick enceinte reinforced by a bastion-like feature exposed by H. de Genouillac along the site's outer perimeter (Tell L), but unfortunately no other information or even a plan of these structures is available.[51]

Excavations in the mound referred to since G. Cros as the *Porte du Diable* (Tell P-P') – apparently for its apotropaic character according to an Arab local legend – and situated in the North-westernmost part of the northern multi-mounded area of the site, revealed the remains of a pre-Sargonic complex-type chambered gate consisting of a straight ca. 3 meter-wide entrance consisting of two sets of buttress-like structures *en vis-à-vis* and flanked by several portions of enceinte, which include casemate-like features and measure ca. 12 meters in width (Fig. 9).[52] In fact, at least two main phases have been posited for the four-pier gate and inner defenses: the first phase probably dating to the reign of Ur-Nanše on the basis of mud-brick dimensions; the second phase perhaps corresponding to the reign of E-anatum on the basis of structural features.[53] Although the later Lagaš II 10 meter-wide rampart constructed during the reign of Gudea from perfectly square-shaped mud-bricks and featuring notably interior and exterior salient buttress-like structures and terracotta inscribed cones has been unearthed by G. Cros in another part of the main temple

---

[50] Cf. Cros, G. 1910, p. 265-276.
[51] Cf. Genouillac, H. de 1936, p. 3.
[52] Cf. Cros, G. 1910, p. 265-276.
[53] Ibid, p. 266.

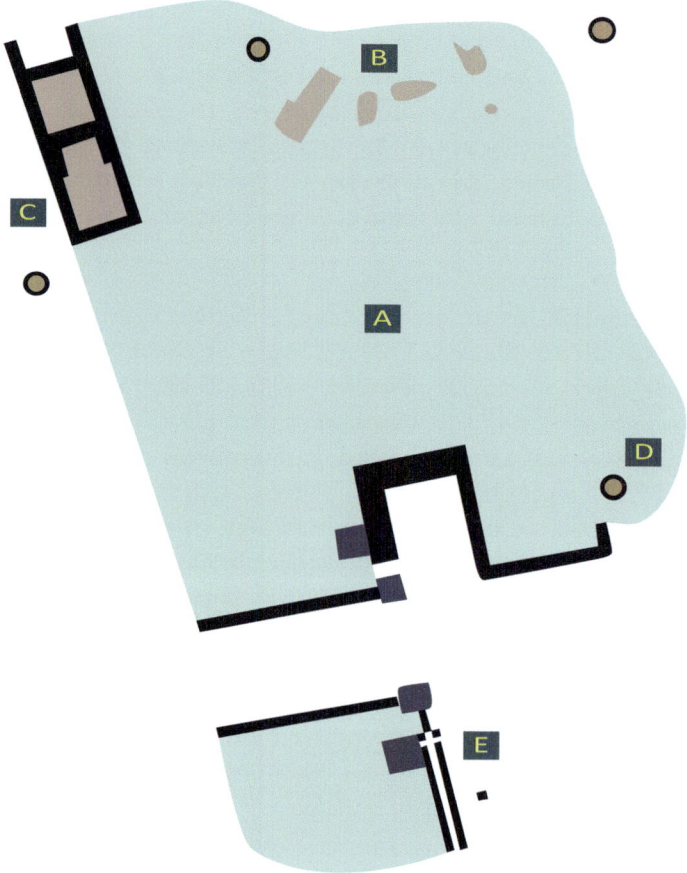

FIG. 9: SCHEMATIC PLAN OF THE EARLY DYNASTIC DEFENDED GATE OF THE MOUND OF THE *PORTE DU DIABLE* (TELL P-P'), EITHER A-BUL₅-LA-ᴅBA-U₂ OR A-BUL₅-LA-ᴅNIN-ĜIR₂-SU, FEATURING (A) THE MUD-BRICK ENCEINTE CA. 12 METER-WIDE (UR-NANŠE/E-ANATUM), (B) COLLAPSED ADOBE STRUCTURES (URUKAGINA), (C) THE SO-CALLED VAULTED CONSTRUCTION, (D) DRAINAGE INSTALLATIONS, AND (E) FIRED-BRICK CANALIZATION.

precinct (Tell I-I'), it likely enclosed the same earlier Lagaš I sacred area and therefore might have been erected directly on the remains of alleged fortification features.[54]

Also, the particular multivallated configuration – that is, multiple-enclosures circumvallating spaces defined by their layouts and functions that differ considerably with one another – may be reflected in the Early Dynastic III textual records. But if the Uruku (iri-ku₃) designating the 'holy quarter' of the city in all likelihood corresponds physically to the major part of the northern district including in particular the first-tier mounds of the *Maison des fruits* (Tell K) and of the Palace (Tell A), it also encompasses in its broadest sense (i.e., probably economically and symbolically after

---

[54] Ibid, p. 305-308; Genouillac, H. de 1936, p. 2-3; Parrot, A. 1948, p. 148.

G. Selz) rural chapels and shrines in the countryside (e.g., the frontier sanctuaries of An-ta-sur-ra and Ti-ra-aš$_2$ nearby the disputed border with Umma).[55] That the Uruku differs from the Eninnu (e$_2$-ninnu) House of Fifty (White *Anzû*-Birds) – that is, the temple precinct of Ningirsu – appears rather self-explanatory, although the relationship between both is rather ambiguous. Yet according to A. Falkenstein, it clearly includes the latter to form a broader religious compound,[56] containing also the temple of Ḫendur-saḡ (the e$_2$-gal-iri-ku$_3$) constructed by En-anatum I,[57] other cultic edifices and storage facilities, such as the e$_2$-ezen-da-iri-ku$_3$, and the e$_2$-u$_4$-sakar-iri-ku$_3$, and, of course, the temple of Ba'u (the e$_2$-TAR-sir$_2$-sir$_2$), constructed by Ur-Nanše.[58]

Administrative tablets from the time of Urukagina's reign (or Iri-KA-gina, Iri'inimgina), which refer to offerings and sacrifices performed during a procession by the queen Sa$_6$-sa$_6$ in the iri-ku$_3$ precinct on the first and last day of the Ningirsu's festival may also point to a multi-tiered organization of the latter.[59] And though philological problems may hamper the understanding of the royal inscriptions and the administrative documents of the First Dynasty of Lagaš – e.g., the identification of certain terms is subject to caution and the translations, to some extant based upon arduous etymological interpretations, have been a matter of scholarly debate – several of the official and archival documents suggest that Presargonic Girsu was enclosed by at least two fortification walls: the bad$_3$ iri-ku$_3$, the 'enceinte of the holy precinct' and the bad$_3$ Ĝir$_2$-su^{ki}, the 'enceinte of the city of Girsu'.

E-anatum's royal inscriptions like that of the present epigraph found on boundary stones and boulders commemorating battles and campaigns directed against Elam, Umma, Uruk, Ur, and other foes, mention that 'He (E-anatum) built the wall of the holy precinct for him (Nin-^{d}ĝir$_2$-su)'.[60] Several other administrative documents of the reign of Urukagina also refer but implicitly to this interior enceinte, dealing precisely with the restoration of the bad$_3$ e$_2$-^{d}Ba-U$_2$ – probably identical with the bad$_3$ iri-ku$_3$ on the basis of a later Gudea royal inscription stating that 'For Ba'u, the beautiful woman, daugther of An, the lady of the Uruku, his lady, Gudea, ruler of Lagaš who had (already) built the Eninnu of Ningirsu, built her wall of the Uruku'.[61] As for the bad$_3$ Ĝir$_2$-su^{ki}, it is only attested in corpora of Urukagina's reign, either in royal inscriptions found on clay cones including a recension of the so-called Reform texts, that is, the above-mentioned reforms carried out by the ruler to correct abuses that had been perpetrated by earlier rulers of Lagaš – 'He (Urukagina) built the wall

---

[55] Cf. Selz, G. 1995, p. 122, 238.
[56] Cf. Falkenstein, A. 1966, p. 121.
[57] Cf. Frayne, D. 2008, p. 171, E1.9.4.2, p. 182, E1.9.4.10. See Selz, G. 1995, p. 143.
[58] Cf. Frayne, D. 2008, p. 114, E1.9.1.29. See Selz, G. 1995, p. 26.
[59] Cf. Rosengarten, Y. 1960, p. 281; Selz, G. 1995, p. 236-238. See Lecompte, C. forthcoming.
[60] Cf. Frayne, D. 2008, p. 147, E1.9.3.5.
[61] Cf. Edzard, D. 1997, p. 111, E3.1.1.7.5.

of Girsu for him (Nin-g̃irsu)' –,[62] on another clay cone stating that 'He encircled Girsu (with a wall) … He made its wall grow up',[63] or on a brick fragment recording the probable restoration or construction of this enceinte.[64]

That the bad$_3$ iri-ku$_3$ and the bad$_3$ G̃ir$_2$-su^{ki} are not one and the same fortification structure (i.e., interchangeable terms) is proven by the fact that both are seemingly attested in contemporaneous epigraphic records of Urukagina's reign, but whether the latter also denotes the entire circumvallated urban space, therefore including the sacred quarter, is a subject of controversy. Patently, the ambiguity arises from the fact that the lines of walling reconstructed from the aerial–satellite imagery and the archeological and survey evidence are contiguous, and in consequence, the portion of plano-convex mud-brick curtain uncovered in the mound of the *Porte du Diable* at the edge of the site (Tell P-P') – also the supposed periphery of the Uruku – is de facto part of the 'enceinte of the holy precinct' as well as that of the 'enceinte of the city of Girsu' on the basis of the above-mentioned inscribed clay cone unearthed in the vicinity.[65] Yet it is clear that the stretch of square-shaped mud-brick curtain, already mentioned, uncovered in the environment of the mound of the *Maison des fruits* at the center of the site (Tell I-I') – even if it dates to the Second Dynasty of Lagaš – may only designate the bad$_3$ iri-ku$_3$ since it yielded numerous terracotta magical cones of Gudea and because of its particular topographic situation.[66]

A thorough morphologic study and ground reconnaissance of the complex of Tello enhanced by analysis of the RAF and Corona imagery led to the identification of several possible defended gates, in addition to the one exposed in the mound of the *Porte du Diable* (Tell P-P'), that overlap the bad$_3$ iri-ku$_3$ and the bad$_3$ G̃ir$_2$-su^{ki}, and are characterized by wide-scale breaks in these otherwise continuous polygonal-type inner and outer defenses.[67] They are frequently situated at the end of the major more or less radial wadi-like ravines of the site and set nearby abutting mounds: at least five have been posited for the sacred precinct (i.e., part of the northern area), and certainly as many, perhaps even more, for the combined elite-related and plebeian large-scale districts (i.e., the most part of the southern area). In the pre-Sargonic epigraphic records – essentially the economic corpus from the queen's manorial estate recently reassessed by C. Lecompte – at least three gates designated as abulla (written in the cuneiform texts as a-bul$_5$-la) and six other as ka$_2$ are attested. And if the former term abulla expressed during the Neo-Sumerian period by the logogram KA$_2$.GAL (the 'great-gate') appears to differ from the latter term (ka$_2$, translated simply 'gate') on the basis of scale and complexity, both may in fact designate in

---

[62] Cf. Frayne, D. 2008, p. 259, E1.9.9.1.
[63] Ibid, p. 276, E1.9.9.4.
[64] Ibid, p. 284, E1. 9.9.10.
[65] Cf. Cros, G. 1910, p. 64.
[66] Ibid, p. 305; Parrot, A. 1948, p. 148. See Lecompte, C. 2014, p. 2.
[67] Cf. Rey, S. & Lecompte, C. in press.

all likelihood in the Presargonic documents the same architectural reality, that is, a defended gate (e.g., the pre-Sargonic ka$_2$-sur-ra is later designated as an abulla-type city gate in the Ur III period).[68]

Of the three recorded a-bul$_5$-la gates in Early Dynastic times – the a-bul$_5$-la-^{d}Ba-U$_2$, the 'gate of Ba'u', the a-bul$_5$-la-^{d}Nin-g̃ir$_2$-su, the 'gate of Ningirsu', and the a-bul$_5$-la-e$_2$-[ki] – only the first two may be speculatively topographically localized: the a-bul$_5$-la-^{d}Ba-U$_2$ in the vicinity of the temple of Ba'u, perhaps West of the so-called mound of the Palace (Tell A), maybe the *Porte du Diable* (Tell P-P'); and the a-bul$_5$-la-^{d}Nin-g̃ir$_2$-su logically nearby the temple of the city-state tutelary deity, that is, in the environment of the mound of the *Maison des fruits* (Tell K). Since such hypotheses remain speculative, it might be that, inversely, the gate excavated in the Tell P-P' matches the a-bul$_5$-la-^{d}Nin-g̃ir$_2$-su. As for the other ka$_2$ gateways, only the ka$_2$-sur-ra can be rather confidently identified with the northeastern entrance of the 'sacred city' (Uruku) – as already posited by G. Cros and L. Heuzey – nearby the so-called mound of the *Grandes briques* (Tell B).[69] As regard to the royal inscriptions, both the Ur-Nanše's limestone slab found at Lagaš commemorating the construction of the Bagara (ba-gara$_2$) temple, and a stone foundation found at Girsu, refer to a rather enigmatic 'Battle gate' (ka$_2$-me), perhaps in reference to a real battle fought by the Lagaš phalanx before a gate of Girsu.[70] Several of Urukagina's official inscriptions merely deal with the social-economic aspects of defended gates: 'He (Urukagina) removed the safe passage toll of the great gate for the pair of workers (…)',[71] another royal inscription – a recension of the ruler's Reform texts – also mentions that 'Indemnity payments for (possession) of stolen goods have been abolished; lost goods are (now) hung at the city gate'.[72]

The Ceremonial Landscape of the City-State's Pantheon

Excavations in the so-called mound of the *Maison des fruits* (Tell K) by E. de Sarzec – the first-tier mound of the site of 14 meters in altitude and covering an area of ca. 6500 square-meters – revealed the remains of a religious complex belonging to Ningirsu, the divine proprietor of the city-state. Probably founded in the Early Dynastic II or IIIa period (i.e., prior to the reign of Ur-Nanše, cf. below), the temple developed in the course of the Early Dynastic III period into a multi-purpose self-contained cultic unit, constructed on a large-scale platform accessible by monumental-like stairways and surrounded by an oval-shaped temenos-enclosure pierced by a simple-type chambered gate; it included the main sanctuary consisting of an enclosed bi-partite rectangular shrine and portico, its corners roughly oriented

---

[68] Cf. Edzard, D. 1997, p. 147, E3.1.1.7.51.10.
[69] Cf. Cros, G. 1910, p. 299.
[70] Cf. Frayne, D. 2008, p. 90-91, E1.9.1.6a, p. 97, E1.9.1.10.
[71] Ibid, p. 264, E1.9.9.1.
[72] Ibid, p. 273, E1.9.9.3.

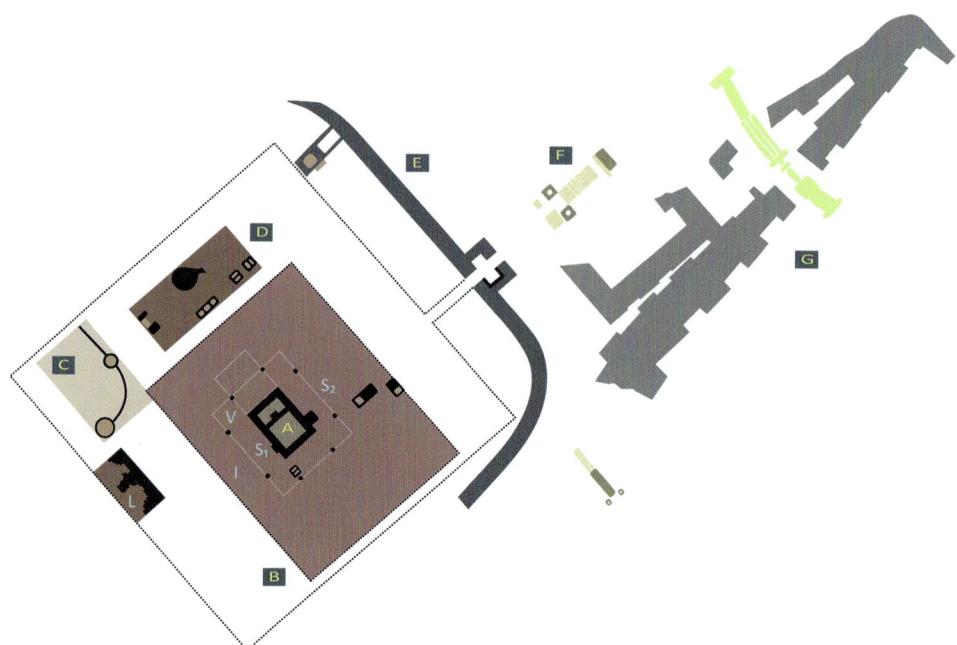

Fig. 10: Schematic plan of the Early Dynastic religious complex of Ningirsu featuring the Construction of Ur-Nanše Eš$_3$-Gir$_2$-su ca. 10 meters by 7 (A), the post-Ur-Nanše cult-platform (B), the well Pu$_2$-šeg$_{12}$ and Kisal-daĝal of E-anatum (C), the Giguna esplanade of En-metena (D), the Oval-wall of the E$_2$-ninnu (E), the Large stairway of Ur-Nanše (F), the Lagaš II temenos-enceinte of Gudea, Bad$_3$ Iri-ku$_3$ (G), and the provenance of ritual artefacts, such as the Stele of the Vultures of E-anatum (S$_1$-S$_2$), the Votive plaque of Ur-Nanše (V), the Inscribed mace of Me-salim (I), and the Liturgical vase of En-metena (L).

to the cardinal points, elevated on a high terrace, and it comprised all the offices, subsidiary services, and other facilities necessary for the cult of the tutelary deity (Fig. 10).[73]

If the sacred precinct and peripheral space also yielded a wealth of truly exceptional monuments of Sumerian art, such as the well-known limestone relief-carved plaque of the *Figure aux plumes*, the Stele of the Vultures, and, thus, has been the subject of a plethora of studies, including on the reconstruction of the immensely problematic stratigraphic pseudo-sequence of temple structures, a lengthy discussion in particular of the latter clearly is beyond the scope of the present book.[74] One may simply recall that at least six main phases pertaining to the Early Dynastic period have been posited for the central area of the mound of the *Maison des fruits*: the first three phases

---

[73] Cf. Sarzec, E. de & Heuzey, L. 1884-1912, p. 68-69, 406-424; Heuzey, L. 1900; Cros, G. 1910, p. 11-15, 68-89; Parrot, A. 1948, p. 54-68.
[74] Cf. Crawford, H. 1987, p. 71-76; Forest, J.-D. 1999, p. 5-31; Huh, S. 2008, p. 83-153; Marchesi, G. & Marchetti, N. 2011, p. 38-44.

belonging to a pre-Dynastic I epoch, the fourth phase may be contemporaneous to the reign of the king (lugal) Me-salim of Kiš (Lugal-ša$_3$-ENGUR ruler (ensi$_2$) of Lagaš), the fifth phase dating to the reign of Ur-Nanše, and the last pre-Sargonic phase corresponding either to a later period of that ruler or perhaps to the reign of E-anatum.

If the above-mentioned hypothesis advanced by A. Falkenstein of a fundamental distinction between the Uruku and the Eninnu appears very likely – that is, the holy precinct spatially encompassing Ningirsu's temple –,[75] it is also clear since A. Parrot on the basis of the cuneiform evidence before the reign of En-anatum I that the latter was called during the reign of Ur-Nanše eš$_3$ G̃ir$_2$-su and e$_2$-^{d}Nin-g̃ir$_2$-su, which might have included or been the *saint des saints* (holy of holies).[76] In fact, the earliest known archaic occurrence of the e$_2$-^{d}Nin-g̃ir$_2$-su may be found on the bas-relief of the *Figure aux plumes*,[77] while the royal inscription of Me-salim of Kiš contemporary of Lugal-ša$_3$-ENGUR incised on a colossal stone mace-head – although referring rather vaguely to several constructions dedicated to Ningirsu – confirms that the development of the Presargonic sacred precinct, is prior to the reign of Ur-Nanše (Fig. 11).[78] Another indication of this terminus ante quem is the discovery under the so-called construction of the latter ruler of several cuneiform tablets dated to the Fāra (ancient Šuruppak) epoch and related to cultic offerings, therefore emphasizing the ancient religious character of the area.[79]

Fig. 11: Mace of Me-salim of Kiš recording the earliest known ruler of Lagaš Lugal-ša-Engur (Sarzec, E. & Heuzey, L. 1884-1912, pl. 1-ter, 2).

Yet clearly Ur-Nanše initiated through the constant remodeling of the precinct an aedilship-kind policy continued by the dynasty's successors that, according to the fist ruler's propagandistic inscriptions, focused especially on the main sanctuary of

---

[75] Cf. Falkenstein, A. 1966, p. 121, 143.
[76] Cf. Parrot, A. 1948, p. 58.
[77] Cf. Gelb, I., Steinkeller, P. & Whiting, R. 1991, p. 67.
[78] Cf. Frayne, D. 2008, p. 70, E1.8.1.1.
[79] Cf. Krebernik, M. 1998, p. 376.

Ningirsu, the eš$_3$-G̃ir$_2$-su/e$_2$-^{d}Nin-g̃ir$_2$-su.[80] However, Ur-Nanše was also responsible for the construction of at least two other important temples in Girsu, the e$_2$-TAR, that is, the temple of Ba'u,[81] probably situated in the Uruku, and equivalent to the later e$_2$-^{d}Ba-U$_2$ renovated by Urukagina, and the šeš-e-g̃ar-ra, the temple of Nanše, originally located outside the boundaries of the 'holy quarter' (Tell L, cf. below).[82] Several other public and secular constructions may also be attributed to his reign on the basis of in situ epigraphic finds, such as the so-called Area of the Basins, and perhaps the *Grand escalier*, the monumental-type stairway leading to the temple of the chief deity Lord of Girsu.[83]

Of the reign of A-kurgal only scarce evidence is available, whereas that of E-anatum yielded a wealth of information related in particular to the plausible enlargement of the religious complex of the mound of the *Maison des fruits* (Tell K): about 25 meters Northwest of the central shrine of the latter E-anatum constructed in Ningirsu's broad courtyard (i.e., the kisal-dag̃al) a large 'brick-(lined) well' (pu$_2$-šeg$_{12}$) made of plano-convex inscribed bricks.[84] Because the kisal-dag̃al is not recorded in Ur-Nanše's royal inscriptions and since E-anatum, as already mentioned, also boasts of having (re)-constructed the 'enceinte of the holy precinct', it appears that in the course of that ruler's reign the Eninnu had probably been considerably restructured. A fragmentary inscription of that ruler on a limestone plaque found during the April 2015 prospection near an archaeological spoil of the Tell K clearly reflects E-anatum's role as a tireless sovereign-builder: ⌈e$_2$-an⌉-[na]-⌈tum$_2$⌉ / P[A.TE.SI] / [Lagaš^{ki}] / dumu A-kur-g[al] / PA.[TE.SI Lagaš^{ki}] (E-anatum, ruler of Lagaš, son of A-kurgal, ruler of Lagaš).[85]

En-anatum I apparently left to posterity only few architectural features, likely responsible for the construction of a terrace situated in the vicinity of the *Grand escalier* (Tell I-I') on the basis of an in situ brick bearing the inscription that 'He (En-anatum I) brought white cedars down to him (Ningirsu) from the mountains. When he had filled in the temple with them he laid its roof thatch (?) of white cedar (branches) for him'.[86]

En-metena's royal inscriptions found on varying types of ex-votos, such as foundation tablets, door-sockets, and bricks, commemorate the construction of the so-called Reed shrine of Ningirsu's Giguna (referred to either as eš$_3$-gi-gi-gu$_3$-ma-^{d}Nin-g̃ir$_2$-su or eš$_3$-gi-^{d}Nin-g̃ir$_2$-su-ka).[87] The latter variant is only attested in one inscription for

---

[80] Cf. Frayne, D. 2008, p. 44, E.1.9.4.7, p. 95, E1.9.4.8, p. 96, E1.9.4.9.
[81] Ibid, p. 114, E1.9.1.29.
[82] Ibid, p. 86, E1.9.1.4, 11, E1.9.1.5, E1.9.1.20, E1.9.1.23, E1.9.1.30a.
[83] Ibid, p. 82, E1.9.1.1.
[84] Cf. Sarzec, E. de & Heuzey, L. 1884-1912, p. 416-419; Frayne, D. 2008, p. 155-158, E1.9.3.9.
[85] Cf. Rey, S., Husain, F. & Lecompte, C. forthcoming.
[86] Cf. Frayne, D. 2008, p. 174, E1.9.4.3.
[87] Ibid, p. 210, E1.9.5.8. See Falkenstein, A. 1966, p. 135.

which five exemplars consisting of bricks have been uncovered, one of them in the so-called Massif of En-metena,[88] while the former occurs in three inscriptions, one of them coming from the so-called Esplanade of En-metena.[89] The Massif of En-metena was probably a large-scale retaining wall or the remains of an earlier cultic platform, located at the westernmost edge of the sacred precinct Eninnu, that is, ca. 15 meters West of the temple of Ur-Nanše, and a few meters South of the well of E-anatum.[90] Also, the Silver vase depicting a representation of the lion-headed eagle (Imdugud), and bearing an inscription of En-metena, and a bitumen stone (possibly slate) recording the temple administrator Dudu's fashioning of a plaque of stone from the city URU×A, both discovered in the area of the Massif of En-metena, were devoted to the patron god of the Eninnu.[91] One may infer that the Eninnu included the Giguna of Ningirsu as was later the case under the reign of Gudea.[92]

As already mentioned, the so-called Esplanade of En-metena included door-socket inscriptions connected with the Giguna shrine. The latter also encompassed a 'brewery' (e_2-bappir) and a 'coach-house' (e_2-^{geš}gigir$_2$-ra) for the god Ningirsu.[93] The fact that inscriptions dealing with the construction of these structures were found in situ North of the temple of Ur-Nanše suggest that they lay close to one another in that area. Also, according to D. Frayne, the e_2-bappir and e_2-^{geš}gigir$_2$-ra of Ningirsu's Giguna may have been restored by Gudea as suggested by a passage in Gudea Cylinder A where mention is made of a nesaĝ, perhaps 'wine-cellar(?)' or 'sacristy', together with a brewery, store-house, and coach-house of the god Ningirsu.[94] A correlation of the En-metena and Gudea corpora would assume that the Gudea inscription contained a topographical description of the temple precinct of Ningirsu. It also coincides with the mention together in Girsu of a 'coach-house' and 'brewery' in an inscription of Urukagina. Also, a clay cone found at Ur (present-day Tell el-Muqayyar) bears an inscription recording En-metena's embellishment of Ningirsu's Eninnu precinct.[95]

Of En-metena's successors only scarce evidence of wide-scale constructions in the cultic district of Girsu is attested until of course the reign of Urukagina.[96] En-anatum II left only one royal inscription on several door-sockets which records the ruler's restoration of a 'brewery' (e_2-bappir) for the god Ningirsu, probably the one already mentioned, constructed by En-metena in the Giguna area. Although a very large number of administrative documents belong to Lugal-Anda's reign, only one

---

[88] Cf. Frayne, D. 2008, p. 212, E19.5.11.
[89] Ibid, p. 210, E1.9.5.8.
[90] Cf. Parrot, A. 1948, p. 65; Forest, J.-D. 1999, p. 17.
[91] Cf. Frayne, D. 2008, p. 232-233, E1.9.5.7 and p. 233, E1.9.5.28.
[92] Cf. Falkenstein, A. 1966, p. 135.
[93] Cf. Frayne, D. 2008 p. 214-215, E.1.9.5.12, for the e_2-bappir p. 217-218, E1.9.5.14, for the e_2-^{geš}gigir$_2$-ra.
[94] Ibid, p. 217.
[95] Ibid, p. 207-208, E1.9.5.6.
[96] Cf. Schrakamp, I. 2015, p. 303-386.

Fig. 12: Artistic view of the Early Dynastic temple of Ningirsu, House of Fifty (White *Anzû*-Birds) by S. Rotella (© Tello-Ancient Girsu Project).

official inscription of that sovereign found on a brick mentions that 'He (Lugal-Anda) erected a monument (stele) and named it Ningirsu is the Lord Eternally Exalted in Nippur'.[97]

Urukagina's royal inscriptions found on stone tablets, door-sockets, and bricks refer to the construction of several shrines inside the Eninnu encompassing the entire mound

---

[97] Cf. Frayne, D. 2008, p. 242-248, E1.9.8.2.

of the *Maison des fruits* (Tell K) as well to a possible restauration of the whole precinct consecrated to Ningirsu,[98] and of the 'coach-house' and 'brewery', both probably located next to the Giguna shrine, North of the inner sanctum of the temple district.[99] The following temples can therefore be located in the 'sacred city' (iri ku$_3$): the shrine of the goddess Ba'u (simply designated by the term e$_2$) probably identical with the e$_2$-tar-sir$_2$-sir$_2$ later mentioned in documents from the time of Gudea,[100] the e$_2$-me-huš-gal-an-ki consecrated to the god Ig-alim,[101] the e$_2$-ki-tuš-akkil-li$_2$-ni, where the god Šul-ša$_3$-ga-na was worshipped,[102] the temple of Lama-sa$_6$-ga, and, within it, the shrines of the divinities Za-za-ru$_{12}$, Ni$_2$-pa-e$_3$ and Ur-nun-ta-e$_3$.[103]

Excavations far beyond the temenos-perimeter of the Ningirsu religious complex of the 'holy city' (Uruku), that is in the so-called mound of the *Logettes vides* (Tell L) in the South-westernmost part of Tello, first by E. de Sarzec, and later by H. de Genouillac revealed, as already noted, East of the likely Early Dynastic archaic enceinte, several mud-brick structures perhaps belonging to a temple construction. The large-scale monument of which unfortunately no plan is available indeed included several inscriptions found on varying types of ex-votos, such as pre-Sargonic bricks and door-sockets, and Ur III clay cones from the time of Šulgi, connected with the construction of the temple of Nanše, called šeš-ğar-ra.[104] Hence, it appears that the temple of Nanše was founded by Ur-Nanše at the periphery of the city, restored by En-metena, and later rebuilt by Šulgi, bearing the name e$_2$-šeš-ğar-ra.

The Logistical Infrastructure of the Ancient Waterways

Several soil marks characteristic of archaic watercourses and paleo-channels have been identified both on the post-World War I aerial photography and the 1968 space imagery of Girsu, and confirmed on the ground in 2015: the main paleo-canal between 15 and 20 meters in width running from Northwest to Southeast on the entire surface of the 'turtleback' and, in the environment of the proper complex of mounds, along the slope of the Eastern tells (i.e., East of the extra-muros district), and other secondary canals of about 10 meters in width situated to the North of the site. Some of these relict hydraulic features likely correspond to the sub-surface traces of the city-harbor and associated waterways reconstructed by G. Cros in the area situated nearby the 'holy city' (iri-ku$_3$), that is, in the vicinity of the so-called mound of the *Grandes briques* (Tell B).[105] That the principal paleo-channel, probably a

---

[98] Ibid, p. 267, E1.9.9.2.
[99] Ibid, p. 280, E1.9.9.6 and p. 281 for the 'coach-house', p. 274, E1.9.9.3 and p. 280, E1.9.9.6 for the 'brewery'.
[100] Ibid, p. 259, E1.9.9.1. According to Genouillac, H. de, 1930a, p. 17-18 and 1930b, p. 170-171 the Ba'u temple may have been situated at the so-called mound of the *Quatre seuils* (Tell G).
[101] Cf. Frayne, D. 2008, E1.9.9.2, p. 267, E1.9.9.3, p. 274, E1.9.9.6, p. 280, E1.9.9.7, p. 281.
[102] Ibid, E1.9.9.2 p. 267, E1.9.9.3, p. 274, E1.9.9.6, p. 281, E1.9.9.7, p. 280, E1.9.9.10, p. 290.
[103] Ibid, E1.9.9.2, p. 267.
[104] Ibid, p. 85-86, E1.9.1.4.
[105] Cf. Cros, G. 1910, p. 64, 298-299.

FIG. 13: THE SO-CALLED ENIGMATIC CONSTRUCTION OF THE EASTERN TELLS, IN FACT A BRIDGE OVER A PALEO-CHANNEL (APRIL 2015).

branch of the ancient Tigris (Idigna), today appears to be raised a few meters above the surrounding plains may be explained because of massive aeolian erosion (i.e., deflation).[106] Careful analysis of its particular course of ca. 3000 meters detectable on RAF and Corona photographs led to the important observation that at the level of present-day Tello this archaic first-tier waterway crossed the Eastern tells roughly from Northwest to Southeast exactly through the so-called *Construction énigmatique* exposed by H. de Genouillac and A. Parrot (Fig. 13).[107]

Excavations in the Eastern tells in the pre-World War II era revealed indeed the remains of this really unique monument of Sumerian public architecture, that is, roughly circumscribed in a ca. 20 by 40 meters rectangular base Northwest-Southeast parallelepiped of about 4 meters in height, possibly constructed in the Early Dynastic period on the basis of plano-convex archaic bricks, and renovated several times in the course of the Ur III and Larsa periods. The epigraphical material, dating only from the Neo-Sumerian period, consists noticeably of a brick of the ruler Pirig̃-me$_3$, which refers to the construction of a weir, Sumerian g̃eš-keš$_2$-ra$_2$,[108] clay cones of Gudea related with the construction of temples dedicated to the divinities Ig-

---

[106] T. Wilkinson & J. Jotheri 2014, pers. comm.
[107] Cf. Genouillac, H. de 1936, p. 16-17; Parrot, A. 1948, p. 211-219.
[108] Cf. Edzard, D. 1997, p. 13, E3.1.1.2.1. See Parrot, A. 1932, p. 55.

FIG. 14: MODERN HIGH RESOLUTION SPACE PHOTOGRAPHY OF TELLO
FEATURING THE MONUMENTAL BRIDGE MADE OF FIRED-BRICKS (A), THE NORTHERN GULLY PERHAPS
THE FERRY TERMINAL KAR-MA$_2$-ADDIR$_x$ (B), THE HOLY-CITY IRI-KU$_3$ (C), THE LINEAR SOIL MARKS OF THE
TEMENOS-ENCEINTE BAD$_3$ IRI-KU$_3$ (D), THE RESIDENTIAL AREAS OF THE LOWER TOWN (E), AND THE PRE-
WORLD WAR II FRENCH ARCHAEOLOGICAL DIG HOUSE (F).

alim and seemingly Šul-ša$_3$-ga-na,[109] a steatite statuette of the human-headed bull dedicated to the ruler Ur-GAR[110] and 90 tablets.[111] If the role of the Enigmatic structure has been a matter of considerable scholarly debate since its discovery – alternately hypogeum, religious complex, reservoir construction, and water regulator –[112] both the re-interpretation by J.-C. Margueron using in particular the 1930 field archives and the objections raised against the previous hypotheses appears rather convincing: the accumulation of alluvial deposits, the structural organization of this large-scale hydraulic feature made of baked-bricks and bitumen, clearly suggest a bridge over a paleo-channel interpretation (Fig. 14).[113]

---
[109] Ibid, p. 162-163, E3.1.1.7.73.
[110] Cf. Parrot, A. 1932, p. 55-56; Edzard, D. 1997, p. 190-191, E3.1.1.9.3.
[111] Cf. Parrot, A. 1932, p. 57.
[112] Cf. Genouillac, H. de 1936, p. 16-17; Parrot, A. 1948, p. 211-219; Jacobsen, T. 1960, p. 174-185; Barrelet, M.-T. 1965, p. 100-118; Pemberton, W. et al. 1988, p. 207-221. See Wilkinson, T. 2013, p. 33-54.
[113] Cf. Margueron J.-C. 2005, p. 63-92.

According to the royal inscriptions and administrative documents of the First Dynasty of Lagaš, the city included a major waterway, the i$_7$-Niĝen$_6^{ki}$-DU-a, the 'Canal which goes (to the city of) Niĝen/Nina (present-day Zurghul)' – the crucial resource and principal lifeline of integration of the Girsu–Lagaš city-state in the pre-Sargonic and Ur III periods – and other secondary canals, including the i$_7$-tur-Ĝir$_2$-su^{ki}-i$_3$-tuku-a, the 'Little Canal which belongs to Girsu'. Urukagina's official inscriptions found on clay cones bearing the recension of the Reform texts mention that: 'For the goddess Nanše, he (Urukagina) dug the Niĝen-DU canal (…), and extended its outlet to the sea'.[114] Furthermore, Urukagina dug for the god Ningirsu the 'Little Canal which belongs to Girsu' and restored its former name, calling it 'the God Ningirsu received (his) authority from Nippur'. He extended it to the Niĝen-DU-a canal'.[115] Also, another royal inscription found on a brick fragment refers to the ruler's construction of a 'reservoir (ĝeš-keš$_2$-ra$_2$) of the 'Canal which goes to Niĝen' (…) out of 432 000 fired bricks and 1820 standard gur saĝ-ĝal$_2$ (2649.6 hectoliters) of bitumen' for the god Ningirsu.[116] Interestingly, this term is identical with the name of the structure built by Piriĝ-me according to the inscription found in the aforementioned monument interpreted as a bridge. The ĝeš-keš$_2$-ra$_2$ built by Urukagina may therefore also designate the bridge.[117]

If the identification of the mega-canal i$_7$-Niĝen^{ki}-DU-a with the Northwest-Southeast major waterway flowing East of present-day Tello – that has been mapped by means of remote-sensing techniques from RAF and Corona photographic interpretations – appears very likely, the localization of the secondary canal i$_7$-tur-Ĝir$_2$-su^{ki}-i$_3$-tuku-a should be subject to caution.[118] Yet, on the basis of its former name, the 'Little Canal which belongs to Girsu', it seems rather likely that this second-tier water-supply feature flowed through part of the city. Perhaps it coincides today with the large-scale wadi-like gully running from North to South in the western part of the site flanked by more or less linear levee-kind features, and precisely in alignment with one of the above-mentioned archaic watercourses identified on the RAF and Corona imagery.

One may argue, moreover, that these rectilinear sorts of embankments bordering the North-South major ravine, Southwest of the 'holy precinct' (iri-ku$_3$), could also be connected to the construction of intramural dykes (Sumerian eg$_2$) recorded in the Early Dynastic cuneiform archives. One tablet of Lugal-Anda's reign mentions the length of 80 ninda-DU (i.e., 480 meters, after re-interpretation of broken cuneiform signs by C. Lecompte) for a dyke (eg$_2$) erected between the bad$_3$ e$_2$-mi$_2$, the 'enceinte of the e$_2$-mi$_2$', that is, the seat of the estate's bureaucratic and ideological apparatus

---

[114] Cf. Frayne, D. 2008, p. 259, E1.9.9.1.
[115] Ibid, p. 265, E1.9.9.1. See Carroué, F. 1986, p. 19.
[116] Cf. Frayne, D. 2008, p. 282-283, E1.9.9.8.
[117] Ibid, p. 148, E1.9.3.5.
[118] Cf. Carroué, F. 1986, p. 15, 19-21.

of the queen Para$_{10}$-nam-tar in the 'sacred city' (iri-ku$_3$) – identical with the later temple of Ba'u (e$_2$-^{d}Ba-U$_2$) –, and the e$_2$-^{d}Nanše; the temple of Nanše, probably identical with the šeš-g̃ar-ra situated, as already mentioned, in the mound of the *Logettes vides* (Tell L).[119] And interestingly enough, the distance between the *Porte du Diable* (Tell P-P'), Northwest of the Uruku religious complex, perhaps the gate of a-bul$_5$-la-^{d}Ba-U$_2$ (the 'gate of Ba'u'), and the šeš-e-g̃ar-ra shrine of Nanše (Tell K), both situated precisely at both ends of the large-scale gully-like feature is about 500 meters.

Other Presargonic epigraphic documents also provide information relating to large-scale hydraulic features connected to the city of Girsu. A pre-Sargonic inscription found on a boulder records various construction works of both En-metena and the temple administrator Dudu, including the kar-ma$_2$-addir$_x$-G̃ir$_2$-su^{ki}, the 'Girsu ferry terminal'.[120] Because on the basis of later Gudea cuneiform sources the principal quay of the city was situated in the vicinity of the ka$_2$-sur-ra defended gate and perhaps the bad$_3$ iri-ku$_3$, the 'enceinte of the holy precinct', it appears likely that from the Early Dynastic period to Ur III times it was situated Northeast of the Uruku exactly in the area where G. Cros identified in 1904 the city-harbor from sub-surface traces. Also, the five perforated cyclopean boulders unearthed by G. Cros Northeast of the so-called mound of the *Grandes briques* (Tell B)[121] – probably proto-anchors for boats (Sumerian ma$_2$) – appear indeed rather comparable to the well-known Byblos and Ugarit stone anchors of respectively the temple of the Obelisks and the temple of Ba'al, and therefore their provenance seems rather consistent with the identification of an archaic port nearby the 'sacred city' (iri-ku$_3$). Perhaps the 'Girsu ferry terminal' (kar-ma$_2$-addir$_x$-G̃ir$_2$-su^{ki}) today topographically corresponds to the northern wide-scale thalweg-kind feature already mentioned above – located between the multi-mounded first-tier complex of the site (Tell A, Tell B, Tell K, Tell I-I', etc.) and the Eastern tells –, and probably connected to one of the secondary paleo-channels detectable on the pre-World War II British air services' photography and the American 1968 space imagery.

---

[119] Cf. Selz, G. 1995, p. 206.
[120] Cf. Frayne, D. 2008, p. 231-232, E1.9.5.27.
[121] Cf. Cros, G. 1910, p. 298-299.

Fig. 15: General layout and topographical features of the Early Dynastic religious megapolis of Girsu reconstructed by combining archaeological and textual evidence and satellite imagery, and confirmed in April and November 2015 by ground reconnaissance: the central sacred precinct (A), the domestic-kind quarters (B), the outer fortifications (C), and the principal paleo-canal (D).

Chapter Three

The Girsu Countryside. The Spatial Organization of a Sumerian City-State

For the goddess Nanše, En-metena, ruler of Lagaš built the E-engur (Temple of the Fountain-head) of the town Zulum; for the goddess Ninḫursag (he) built the Giguna (Multi-colored Reeds) of the shinning grove; for the god Ningirsu (he) built the boundary town of Antasura (whose) temple's awesome splendor covers all the lands.[122]

The Myth of the Sumerian Archaic Agrotown

Seeking to reconstruct by means of a multifaceted ecological approach the patterns of ancient occupancy in the Mesopotamian floodplain, particularly the rural landscape of the first cities, R. Adams, H. Nissen, and other scholars carried out in 1960-70 broad-scale ground prospections identifying archaeological sites and remnants of archaic waterways that connected the latter. These regional surveys were truly ground-breaking because they completely shifted the focus from the temples and clay tablets – i.e., 'from a city-centered view' – to the countryside, 'the rural settlements and irrigation agriculture that produced and sustained the city'.[123] They led to the development of a chronological sequence or sequential model of the rise of the Sumerian state that, as pointed out be P. Steinkeller,[124] has become a historiographical cornerstone: (1) first a steady growth of protohistoric agglomerations throughout the second half of the 4th Millennium (Late Uruk); (2) followed by a rapid growth (or explosion) of urban centers at the beginning of the 3rd Millennium (Jemdat Nasr-Early Dynastic I); (3) this happened at the expense of rural settlements which apparently almost completely disappeared; (4) and in turn led to the formation of the Classical Sumerian Agrotowns or city-based agrarian states of the Early Dynastic II-III period.

More specifically, on the basis of the results from the surface survey in the region around Uruk, while in Late Uruk times the ratio between villages on the one hand and towns, small urban centers, and cities on the other appeared to be 112 to 11, the proportion developed to 124 to 23 in the Jemdat Nasr-ED I period, and to 17 to 16 for the ED II-III period.[125] Accordingly, rural sites represented extremely rare features in the general pattern of Presargonic occupancy. And at the apex, in R. Adams and H. Nissen own terms: 'Uruk (already a flourishing theocratic center) attained its

---

[122] Cf. Frayne, D. 2008, p. 214-2015, En-metena E1.9.5.12.
[123] Cf. Adams, R. & Nissen, H. 1972; Adams, R. 1981.
[124] Cf. Steinkeller, P. 2007, p. 186-187.
[125] Cf. Adams, R. & Nissen, H. 1972, p. 18.

FIG. 16: THE IMMEDIATE HINTERLANDS OF GIRSU. ARCHAEOLOGICAL MOUNDS OF TELLO ARE DETECTABLE IN THE BACKGROUND (NOVEMBER 2015).

largest urbanized area during the ED I period, but thereafter its ascendancy was increasingly challenged by the growth of a number of other city-states of rival size. This trend continued through the end of the Early Dynastic period, leading to the aggregation of the great majority of the region's population within walled centers of unquestionably urban proportions'.[126] After R. Adams scholars like M. Liverani characterized the Sumerian landscape 'landmarked by large cities that burn out (so to speak) the surrounding villages'.[127]

Yet also concentrating on the topics of rural settlements and the relationship between urban centers and their countryside in Southern Babylonia, especially the topography of the province of Umma in Ur III times (2100-2000 BC), P. Steinkeller's seminal research led to reevaluate the long-lasting model of the city-based agrarian state demonstrating the importance of villages' networks.[128] Relying on a single archive of about 15 000 cuneiform tablets, P. Steinkeller compiled a catalog of 110 settlements

---

[126] Ibid. p. 19.
[127] Cf. Liverani, M. 1999, p. 45.
[128] Cf. Steinkeller, P. 2007, p. 185-211.

confidently assigned to the province of Umma. By establishing a four-rank typology on the basis of various size indicators, such as the site size as determined through archaeological surface survey, the presence of textually documented architectural features within a settlement, the titles and professional designations of individuals associated with a settlement, the population, the settlement's general reputation, and the toponym of the settlement itself, he proved that the province of ca. 2000 square-kilometers included a prime city (the eponymous province capital Umma), 12 towns, 12 small towns / large villages, and 85 small villages or hamlets.[129] P. Steinkeller consequently refuted the prevailing view of a dichotomy between the urban and rural spheres in Early Mesopotamia – the 'predatory posture of cities on their hinterlands' – arguing on the contrary for the existence of a 'high degree of connectedness and mutual dependence' among settlements of all types: 'rather than representing two different, sharply contrasted phenomena, (he wrote) at Umma the urban city and its countryside form a continuum, as regards both the physical and the socioeconomic landscape'.[130] To be sure a radical change of perspective.

The Regional Setting of an Early Dynastic City-State

In the wake of P. Steinkeller's pivotal study, C. Lecompte, by re-examining the Presargonic agro-managerial archives of the last queens of Lagaš I, has likewise pointed out the high density of rural habitats scattered throughout the hinterland of Girsu in the Early Dynastic period.[131] Adopting a comparable approach of establishing a typology based on a variety of criteria like the settlement's toponym (and its permanence in corpora of later periods), the nature of the settlement (its economical functions), the profession of individuals or corporations connected to the settlement, the network of rural places, the geographical location, architectural super-structures, the reputation of the settlement, C. Lecompte managed to prove moreover the frequent equivalence of the term e_2 from Presargonic tablets in nonurban context to that of e_2-duru$_5$ of Ur III times precisely designating a village.[132] Although e_2 generally equate with households, temples in urban context, cuneiform tablets from Nippur include e.g. several toponyms e_2 attested with the post-determinative [ki] of places, such as e_2-Ma-ma^{ki} or e_2-luḫ-ḫu^{ki}.[133]

Dozens of e_2 rural settlements like, e.g the well-attested E_2-ki-sal$_4$-la, appear in the Lagaš I archives from Girsu.[134] The toponym E_2-ki-sal$_4$-la refers to both a storehouse (e_2) and the place Ki-sal$_4$ located along the Salla canal North of Girsu. It was in all likelihood connected to the later town of A-pi$_4$-sal$_4$ in Ur III times and probably a

---

[129] Ibid, p. 196.
[130] Ibid, p. 201.
[131] Cf. Lecompte, C. 2015, p. 211-246.
[132] Ibid, p. 214-218.
[133] Cf. Westenholz, A. 1975, p. 111.
[134] Cf. Lecompte, C. 2015, p. 219-223.

first-tier granary because large amounts of barley and other products were stored for the cult and offerings as well as agricultural tools for the harvest. It appears to have been managed directly by a high official (Sumerian nu-banda$_3$) of the e$_2$-mi$_2$ / e$_2$-^{d}Ba'u. Hence the place E$_2$-ki-sal$_4$-la was very likely a large rural settlement and a first-tier agricultural center.[135] That another place E$_2$-ma-nu, also a Presargonic village attested as E$_2$-duru$_5$-ma-nu in the Ur III period, probably a storage facility, was apparently connected to the settlement E$_2$-ki-sal$_4$-la seems to point furthermore to a network of large farms, storehouses, granaries in the Girsu countryside.[136] Localities such as E$_2$-bar-^{d}Bil$_3$-aga$_3$-mes-še$_3$-du$_3$-a (the Abode built nearby the temple of Gilgameš) or E$_2$-bar-Ti-ra-aš$_2^{ki}$ (literally the Abode outside Ti-ra-aš$_2^{ki}$) also appear to have been rural settlements and, in the latter, also a storage place primarily for reed located in the close vicinity of a town.[137]

Other structures like ĝanun nonurban storehouses and bad$_3$ rural watch-towers connected to fields or fortified farms occur though rarely in the Presargonic epigraphical records like, e.g. bad$_3$ aša$_5$ da-UL$_4$, bad$_3$ aša$_5$ me-dib situated in the neighborhood of Girsu.[138] Nonurban chapels and shrines on the other hand are well attested in offering lists recording libations and sacrifices for the Lagaš pantheon.[139] Several rural sanctuaries dedicated to specific gods only included a clergy connected to the cult: e.g., the Nanše temple E$_2$-engur-ra-(aša$_5$)-zu$_2$-lum (Engur temple of (the field) zu$_2$-lum) appears to have been managed by two priests (Sumerian gala) and was located nearby Lagaš.[140] Regular offerings were delivered to the Ib-i$_7$-edin-na (Oval temple of the canal of the steppe) probably located in the northwestern area of Girsu. Likewise a few of the abzu nonurban temples may have been situated nearby Girsu (e.g., Abzu-iri-sig-ba, the Abzu of the suburb).[141]

Secondary towns or small urban centers that differ from large villages predominantly because of their reputation, the high role of the personnel connected to them, the presence of prime architectural features, may also be approximately geographically located in the Girsu countryside. UM^{ki} and Utul$_2$-gal^{ki} are for instance mainly attested in cult personnel lists (gala priests connected to them) reflecting therefore their important regional role as probable religious centers, the latter including moreover the temple complex E$_2$-dam.[142] Other comparable hubs were the well-known localities of Antasura, Ambar/Tir-ambar^{ki} and Ti-ra-aš$_2^{ki}$. The presence of a high temple administrator (Sumerian saĝĝa) naturally points to the importance of the agglomeration in the territorial organization of the state: the saĝĝa of ^{d}Nin-MAR.KI

---

[135] Cf. Carroué, F. 1983, p. 97-112.
[136] Cf. Lecompte, C. 2015, p. 223.
[137] Cf. Selz, G. p. 1998, p. 106.
[138] Cf. Lecompte, C. 2015, p. 225-227.
[139] Cf. Selz, G. 1998, p. 122.
[140] Ibid, p. 210.
[141] Ibid, p. 122; Lecompte, C. 2015, p. 227.
[142] C. Lecompte, pers. comm.

a district center located in the Gu'abba area South of Lagaš managed e.g. to gather during the reign of En-anatum II a large force from the neighborhood of the town to fightback an Elamite raid.

Likewise the presence of large-scale recorded architectural features within a settlement certainly suggests their prime role, either at managerial or symbolic level, or both. URU×KAR$_2$ /Uru$_{11}$ another large town nearby Lagaš considered to be the principal center of cult of the god Lugal-uru$_{11}$ featured at least a 'palace' (e$_2$-gal) for its tutelary deity (probably a sanctuary) and a very large storehouse, the ĝanun-mah, and was managed by a saĝĝa governor flanked by a herald (niĝir). Regarding the environs of Girsu proper, at least E$_2$-babbar$_2$ appears to have held the role of second-tier center: it included a bad$_3$ defended enceinte, a saĝĝa archpriest as superintendent, and several other lesser officials (gala, gudu$_4$).[143]

As for the first-tier ceremonial centers of the Early Dynastic city-state – except Girsu (Tello) whose topography seems rather clear – only scarce textual information pertains in fact to the two other largely urbanized areas of Lagaš (al-Hiba) and Niĝen (Zurghul).[144] At Lagaš only temples like the Ibgal dedicated to the goddess Inanna, the Šapada for the goddess Nanše, and the Bagara of the god Ningirsu, as well as a few storage structures, and a fortification feature (bad$_3$ Lagaš^{ki}) are attested. On the basis of Presargonic sources alone Niĝen appears in effect as a mere city of shrines: E$_2$-mah, E$_2$-^{d}Nanše, Nin-ne$_2$-ĝar-ra.[145]

Overall, the thorough re-investigation of the Lagaš I cuneiform tablets by C. Lecompte led to a five- or perhaps six-tier complex settlement pattern: the city-state centered on Girsu's sacred precinct Uruku incorporated a triad of first-tier urban centers, 14 important cultic places, secondary towns, and/or district centers, plus 9 places corresponding probably also to prime settlements, 5 large villages, 12 rural chapels or shrines, 37 small villages, hamlets, nonurban granaries, and watch-towers.[146] As suggested by P. Steinkeller: 'Sumerian city-states clearly were based on a high level of social and economic integration between towns and the countryside'.[147]

Surveying the region around Girsu in 1969 T. Jacobsen had already stressed the importance of Protodynastic archaeological sites in the territory especially the Gu'edena border with the rival city-state of Umma (present-day Jokha).[148] Yet the results of that area's surface reconnaissance summarily published in *Sumer* were largely neglected by Mesopotamian scholars probably overshadowed by the regional

---

[143] Cf. Lecompte, C. 2015, p. 232.
[144] Cf. Carroué, F. 1983, p. 97-112.
[145] Cf. Lecompte, C. 2015, p. 234.
[146] Ibid, p. 236.
[147] Cf. Steinkeller, P. 2007, p. 205.
[148] Cf. Jacobsen, T. 1969, p. 103-109.

surveys of R. Adams. The Tello field-prospection led to the identification of relict hydraulic features, archaic waterways, and about 40 Early Dynastic sites based on pottery seriation, all in all a complex pattern of occupancy throughout part of the Girsu countryside. Of course the reconstruction of T. Jacobsen proposing to connect the topographical features identified on the ground to well-known settlements and canals from the epigraphical records remains tentative or to some degree rather speculative. Many 3rd Millennium archaeological ruins may well have been buried under the alluvial depositional layers of the present-day Shatt al-Gharraf and its effluents, one of the marsh-feeding Tigris distributaries.[149]

Since the first ground prospections of Southern Babylonia important conceptual advances in remote sensing techniques have occurred – largely embodied in the research of T. Wilkinson who argued that once properly geo-rectified and scrutinized, aerial or satellite datasets permit highly detailed and accurate mapping, and as a result significantly enhance earlier surface reconnaissance.[150] Though the Girsu territory on the whole has thus far received relatively brief topographical scrutiny (in comparison to other Mesopotamian areas), the analysis in particular of the Cold War-era space photographs sheds new light on its organization. Corona imagery taken in 1968, i.e., at about the same time as T. Jacobsen's reconnaissance, preserves moreover a picture of the landscape prior to large-scale transformations of the post-1960 Arab agrarian revolution (urban expansion, agricultural intensification, reservoir construction), even if the Sumerian plain appears in fact as a palimpsest of superimposed landscapes.

Yet as suggested by T. Wilkinson, the 1968 Corona imagery has significantly enhanced the 1969 Tello regional survey. Many if not most of the Early Dynastic sites have been re-analyzed and re-mapped by means of remote-sensing techniques from georeferenced photographic interpretations (Fig. 17). Hence, the particular spatial organization depicting an important density of sites and canalization, consequently also sedentary occupation and population, re-interpreted on the basis of an interdisciplinary approach corresponds to the rather complex setting of the city-state partially reconstructed from Lagaš I cuneiform tablets. It is therefore possible to plot the textually recorded settlements and watercourses re-assessed by C. Lecompte within the borders of the Girsu countryside using the geo-corrected map of T. Jacobsen as a base reference against previous sketches of both the Early Dynastic city-state and the Ur III province.[151]

Thanks to the wealth of information relating particularly to the geographical context of these features provided by the Presargonic Ba'u archives – and after cross-checking the data – the rural habitats and hydraulic features can indeed be

---

[149] Cf. Wilkinson, T. 2013, p. 33-54.
[150] Cf. Wilkinson, T. 2003.
[151] Cf. Huh, S. 2008, p. 1-17.

The Girsu Countryside. The Spatial Organization of a Sumerian City-State

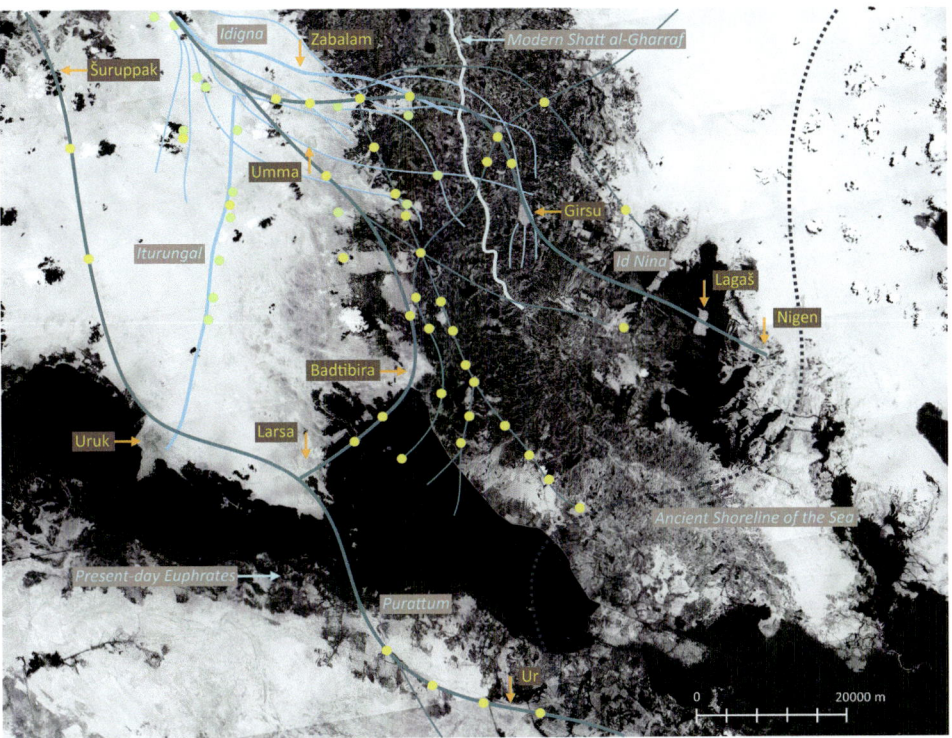

FIG. 17: SUPERIMPOSED 1968 CORONA SPACE PHOTOGRAPHY OF SOUTHERN BABYLONIA WITH THE T. JACOBSEN 1969 MAP OF EARLY DYNASTIC SITES, CANALS, AND ANCIENT RIVERS IN THE GIRSU REGION (P. 109), AND THE R. ADAMS 2008 RE-ASSESSED MAP OF UR III SITES AND WATERCOURSES IN THE UMMA REGION (P. 7).

approximatively mapped in polygons and ovals of varying sizes. I have adopted a somewhat pragmatic approach hierarchizing the information as far as possible. Hence the overlying shapes' sizes differ depending on the reliability of the data in order to reduce naturally the margin of error. Each archaeological site corresponding to a well-known recorded Early Dynastic first- or second-tier locus features a polygon: obviously Tello-Girsu, al-Hiba-Lagaš, Zurghul-Niĝen, but also Antasura-Imrebi'a and Ekisal (equal to Ur III Apisal)-Muhalliqiya. Consequently all settlements located nearby or in the outskirts of these centers have been placed therein: e.g., the town Ki-nu-nir^{ki} probably located just North of Lagaš or the suburban chapel Abzu-iri-sig Northwest of Girsu. Other settlements merely located against a cardinal point with respect to a prime city or in the rather well delineated sub-regional areas like the Gu'edena or the Gu'abba are positioned in overlapping ovals generated empirically throughout the territory: e.g., the border fort Bad$_3$ da-Sal$_4$-la situated in the Gu'edena or the walled-sanctuary A-Huš Northwest of Lagaš.

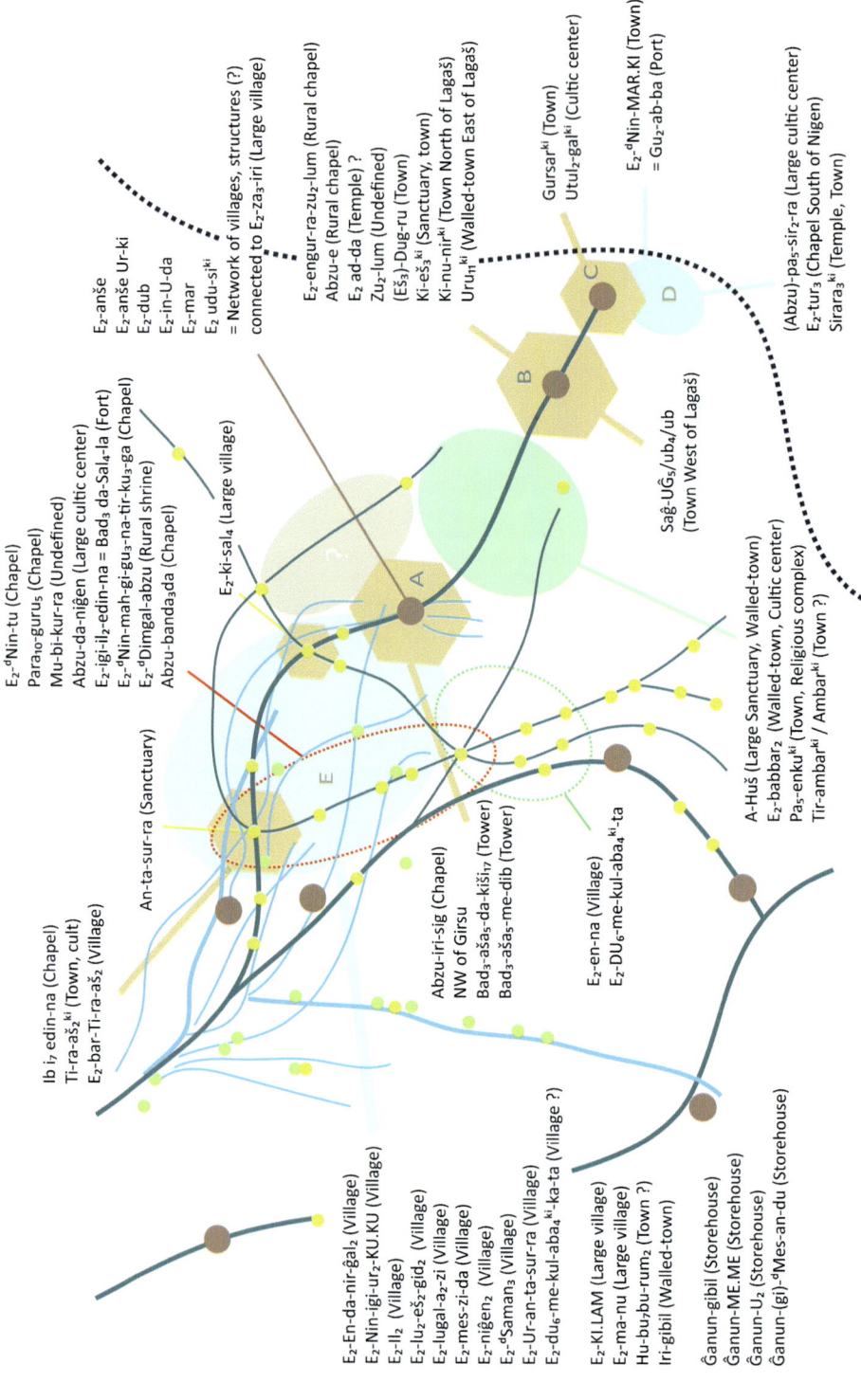

Fig. 18: Map of the Early Dynastic settlement pattern of the Girsu-Lagaš city-state highlighting (a) the region around Girsu, (b) the Lagaš neighborhood, (c) the Niĝen district, (d) the Gu'abba area, and (e) the Gu'edena border.

Overall, about 60 places or toponomys of cities, towns, villages, rural shrines, nonurban towers, have been approximatively located within these polygons and ovals (Fig. 18). It appears therefore clear that, like for the Umma province in Ur III times, the centers of Girsu, Lagaš, and Niğen and their hinterlands formed a continuum in the Early Dynastic period. Also, as already stressed, the state's principal watercourse – the Canal going to Niğen – crossing it from Northwest to Southeast precisely through the urban triad provided a connective nexus in an enclosing network of waterways serving the other settlements of the city-state.[152] Several of these secondary hydraulic features well-attested in the epigraphical records have also been tentatively plotted, such as the I$_7$-nun canal, the I$_7$-Ambar canal, the Boundary canal Eg$_2$-mah-ki-sur-ra in the Gu'edena, as well as the ancient marshes such as the Ambar-Lagaš^{ki} and Ambar-Nigen$_6^{ki}$ located nearby or within the Gu'abba in the southeastern part of the territory (Fig. 19).

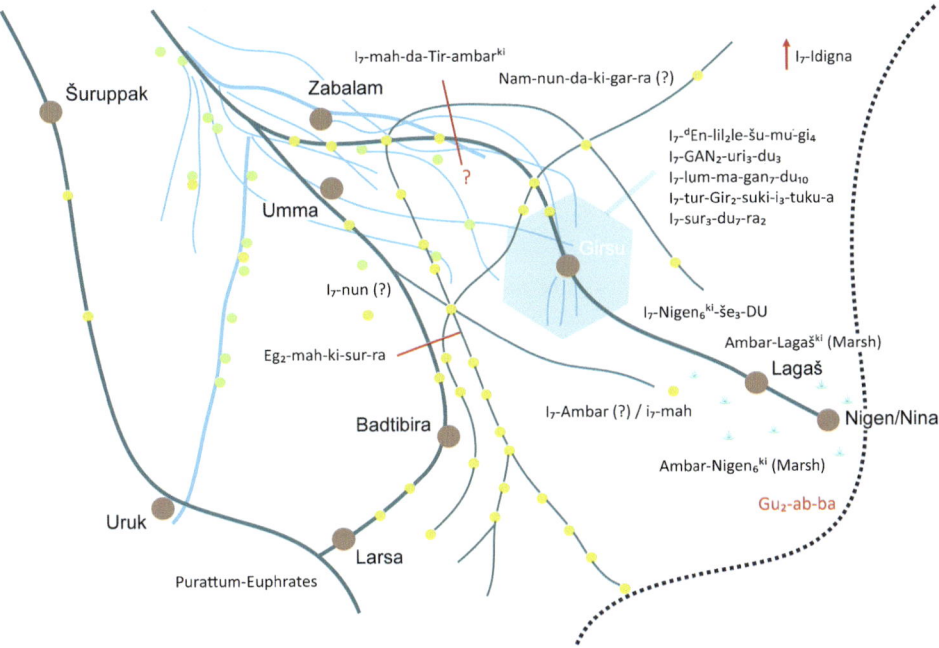

FIG. 19: MAP OF THE EARLY DYNASTIC NETWORK OF WATERCOURSES AND MARSHLANDS OF THE GIRSU-LAGAŠ CITY-STATE.

The Ritual Processions in Honor of the Gods

Religion and especially pilgrimage rites across the countryside have long been considered by Mesopotamian scholars as a chief element in the complex process

---
[152] Cf. Wilkinson, T. 2013, p. 33-53.

of early state formation in Ancient Sumer. While R. Adams forcefully argued for 'a primarily religious focus to social life at the outset of the Urban Revolution',[153] P. Steinkeller stated that 'it was indeed religion (specifically: cult) that cemented and perpetuated social and economic relationships between the settlements within individual city-sates'.[154] The reinvestigation of the rich archives of the Lagaš I queens (in the reigns of Lugal-Anada and Urukagina) by G. Selz and especially C. Lecompte have led moreover to reconstruct ritual processions throughout the Girsu-Lagaš countryside during yearly cultic celebrations of the city-state in honor of its pantheon, Ningirsu, Ba'u, Nanše, which clearly had the purpose of establishing a form of territorial unity through cult.[155] Mapping these ceremonial routes or cultic-ways provides therefore significant insights into the sacral geography of the Presargonic city-state (Fig. 20).

The principal religious feast in honor of the state's patron-god Ningirsu, probably carried out twice a year on the basis of offering lists (i.e., in the months of iti ezem še gu$_7$ ^{d}Nin-ĝirsu and iti ezem munu$_4$ gu$_7$ ^{d}Nin-ĝirsu, corresponding to the months 1 / 4 (?) and 9 / 10 of the Lagaš religious calendar) lasted three of four days according to the archival corpuses recording the expenses for sacrifice.[156] The procession started in the sacred precinct of Girsu (Uruku), traversed the territory towards the Gu'edena passing by shrines (e.g., Ib-i$_7$-eden-na, Tir-ra-aš$_2$, Abzu-da-niĝen) and returned to the city-sate's religious center Uruku on the last day of the festival. Daily sacrifices and ritual libations to the tutelary god may have accompanied the entire pilgrimage either in rural chapels or open-field consecrated places, some located at the frontier, but the principal purpose of the ritual procession was the border sanctuary of Antasurra, the primary nonurban temple of Ningirsu.

During the festival of the goddess Ba'u that lasted four days at the time of Urukagina, a nonurban procession led by the queen Sasa circumvallated part of the Girsu western border stopping at sanctuaries like the Ib-i$_7$-eden-na (the Oval of the steppe's canal) and other chapels in the environs of Badtibira that had been conquered by En-metena but lost by the last rulers of Lagaš.[157] The feast in honor of the goddess Nanše, venerated at Niĝen, carried out during the so-called 'months of the consumption of barley (or malt) festival of Nanše' (iti ezem še gu$_7$ ^{d}Nanše and iti ezem munu$_4$ ^{d}Nanše), and coinciding with the months 1 / 2 and 8 / 9 of the local calendar, lasted 6 to 8 days.[158] The procession started at Girsu traversed the countryside towards Lagaš where offerings were performed in the Šapada, Ibgal, and Bagara temples, then headed to Niĝen, of course the prime locus of the ritual

---

[153] Cf. Adams, R. 1966, p. 121.
[154] Cf. Steinkeller, P. 2007, p. 206.
[155] Cf. Selz, G. 1995; Lecompte, C. forthcoming.
[156] Cf. Selz, G p. 237.
[157] Ibid, p. 32-36.
[158] Cf. Rosengarten, 1960, p. 418.

The Girsu Countryside. The Spatial Organization of a Sumerian City-State

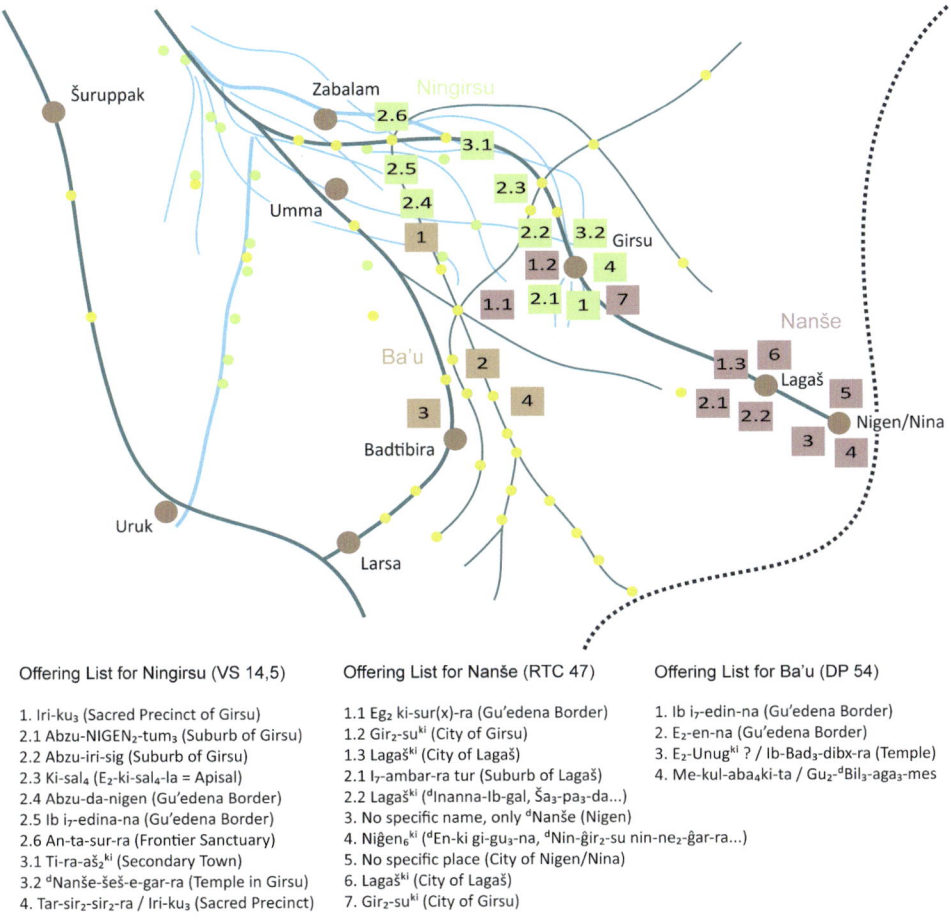

FIG. 20: RECONSTRUCTION OF THE EARLY DYNASTIC RITUAL PROCESSION-WAYS OF THE GIRSU-LAGAŠ CITY-STATE FROM OFFERING LISTS RECORDING LIBATIONS AND SACRIFICES FOR THE GODS NINGIRSU, NANŠE, AND BA'U.

and where probable ceremonial banquets were held to worship Nanše, and returned to Girsu on the last day after a stop at Lagaš. Other feasts honoring lesser gods of the city-state have also been reconstructed on the basis of offering lists, such as the procession for the god Nin-MAR.KI in the Gu'abba region facing the sea.[159]

The Sacred Precinct and Central Cult of the City-State

Because of the importance of pilgrimage rituals in the sociopolitical constitution of the nascent Girsu-Lagaš city-state, especially the popular feasts in honor of the

---
[159] Cf. Selz, G. 1995, p. 257-258.

FIG. 21: GENERAL VIEW OF THE SACRED PRECINCT OF GIRSU (NOVEMBER 2015) FEATURING THE ARCHAEOLOGICAL SPOILS OF THE MOUND OF THE PALACE (A), AREA A AT THE CENTER OF THE HOLY-CITY IRI-KU$_3$ (B), THE LINEAR LEVEE-KIND FEATURE CORRESPONDING TO THE REMAINS OF THE EARLY DYNASTIC TEMENOS-WALL (C), THE RESIDENTIAL AREAS FEATURING DOMESTIC-TYPE SURFACE ARTEFACTS (D), THE PERIPHERAL TELL L, PROBABLY THE ŠEŠ-E-ĞAR-RA SHRINE OF NANŠE (E), THE LOCATION OF THE FORMER MOUND OF THE *MAISON DES FRUITS* (TELL K), THE PRESARGONIC E$_2$-NINNU TEMPLE (F), AND THE HEAPS OF EARTH NEARBY TELL I-I', THE LAGAŠ II SACRED-ENCEINTE OF GUDEA (G).

supernatural overlord, and since the focal point of these circumambulatory regional processions appears to be the Uruku of Girsu, the choice to open a new excavation at Tello in November 2015 (80 years after A. Parrot's last field-campaign) fell on the central area of the sacred precinct already reconstructed from a many-sided approach and thoroughly surveyed in April 2015.

To be sure the search of the sacred center – rarely equivalent to the geographical center in Ancient Sumer – proved not to be self-evident primarily because of the presence of giant heaps of spoils and archaeological pits. Area A has been established therefore on the basis of a preliminary morphological study of the large-scale complex of mounds enhanced by remote sensing techniques and ground reconnaissance (Fig. 21). Located in the environs of the intersection point of the two principal structuring axes of the Uruku walled-precinct connecting from North to South the Mound of the Palace (Tell A) to the Mound of the *Maison des fruits* (Tell K), and from East to West the Mound of the *Quatre seuils* (Tell G) to the Mound of the *Porte du Diable* (Tell P-P'), Area A clearly occupies a focal position. Furthermore the large ravines (or gullies) of the area detectable from space and confirmed on the ground, corresponding in all likelihood to the ancient streets of the holy quarter that connected the temples and their annexes, all appear to radiate from this pivotal pole. At the end of the alleged pathways were probably located the gates of the sacred precinct, such as the already exposed *Porte du Diable* (Tell P-P').

Although topographically situated between 8 and 10 meters above the flat alluvial neighboring lands (on the basis of the first contour map produced by E. de Sarzec), that is, about 3 to 5 meters above the presupposed residential areas of the lower town beyond the temenos-enceinte, Area A lies in fact a few meters below the first-tier surrounding mounds (Tell A, Tell K) in a sort of artificial depression suggesting therefore a particular purpose at the town-planning or urbanization level and a specific role as regards the religious scenography of the sacred precinct. Another important hint to the rather peculiar character of the central crater-like area can be extrapolated in fact from the previous field-work of the French-led expeditions, especially the soundings carried out by G. Cros in 1903 in the near vicinity of the Area of the Basins (so-called Vale between the tells) that revealed according to the latter's own report: 'only a large open space which sloped northward and towards the part of the plain located between the Mound of the *Maison des fruits* and the Mound of the Palace. In this area (he wrote) no construction of any significance has been discovered'.[160] Understandably the apparent poor results of G. Cros' trenches nearby Area A precluded (perhaps all the better) any further archaeological reinvestigations of the central sacred precinct by H. de Genouillac or A. Parrot between 1929 and 1933.

Excavations in Area A in November 2015 revealed directly below the surface well-preserved archaeological features dating to the Early Dynastic period on the basis of the pottery. Later phases corresponding to Lagaš II and Ur III times had been completely eroded: only a few lost relics of Gudea's dynasty including fragments of inscribed bricks emerged from the battered topsoil. The Presargonic level exposed over an area of 500 square-meters consisted of a large open space composed of an earthen floor including a large amount of well-known ED III ceremonial feasting terracotta vessels. The square extending thus over the entire surface of Area A comprised at least two circular terracotta structures about 30 meters apart composed of multiple interlocked ceramic cylinders of 60 cm in diameter fitted vertically one within the other to form drainage installations for the evacuation of rain water and other detritus. It also included eight quadrangular and oval-shape structures filled with ash ranging from 20 to 40 cm long and from 15 to 30 cm large consisting

---

[160] Cf. Cros, G. 1910, p. 108.

FIG. 22: THE EARLY DYNASTIC CEREMONIAL PLAZA OF THE SACRED PRECINCT OF GIRSU (AREA A EXCAVATED IN NOVEMBER 2015 BETWEEN THE MOUND OF THE *MAISON DES FRUITS* AND THE MOUND OF THE PALACE, G) FEATURING SUPERIMPOSED EARTHEN FLOORS AND BURNT LAYERS (A), THE LARGE OPEN SPACE INCLUDING ED III FEASTING TERRACOTTA VESSELS (B), BROKEN GOBLETS FROM A FAVISSA (C), ASHY LAYERS, PROBABLY THE REMNANTS OF LARGE RITUAL FIRES (D), A LIBATION VASE NEARBY A TERRACOTTA DRAIN (E), ANOTHER DRAIN AND SEVERAL TERRACOTTA FLOOR LAMPS (F).

of fired bricks set on the edge or made entirely of terracotta, in fact hearths in all likelihood for lighting, i.e., ancient lanterns or floor lamps. In places, the plaza's adobe floor featured relatively thick ashy layers, probably the remnants of large ritual fires as proven by the presence of a favissa partly excavated in a sounding originally opened in order to establish the stratigraphy of the ceremonial square. The trench revealed a long sequence of superimposed earthen floors and burnt layers cut by the 2.50 meter-deep favissa or ritual pit packed with more than 250 ceremonial terracotta broken cups or goblets probably used in a religious feast and thereafter ritually discarded, and a large quantity of fauna bones, also the remnants of a banquet or sacrifice (Fig. 22).

Predictably the sacred open space yielded predominately three types of ED III pottery approximatively in decreasing percentage: goblets (60), bowls (20), spouted jars (10), and other (10) including a large cultic vase 30 centimeters high for offerings or libations apparently diagnostic of the late ED III period (or perhaps ED IIIb/

FIG. 23: EARLY DYNASTIC III CEREMONIAL TERRACOTTA VESSELS FROM AREA A (CUP H. 15 CM, LIBATION VASE H. 34 CM) DEPICTED ON THE PLAQUE OF UR-NANŠE COMMEMORATING THE RELIGIOUS DEED OF THE RULER PRESIDING OVER THE RITUALS OF (RE)FOUNDATION OF THE ENINNU SANCTUARY (SARZEC, E. & HEUZEY, L. 1884-1912, PL. 2-BIS, 1) AND THE LIBATION PLAQUE FROM UR REPRESENTING RELIGIOUS PROCESSIONS LED BY PRIESTS POURING OFFERINGS IN FRONT OF A GOD AND A TEMPLE AND FOLLOWED BY WORSHIPPERS (© TRUSTEES OF THE BRITISH MUSEUM, 2016).

proto-Imperial transitional phase) and therefore dating the ceremonial place probably to the reign of the last Lagaš I ruler Urukagina at the time of Lugul-zagesi and Sargon of Akkad.[161] Of course the assemblage of cups, bowls, and spouted jars, and the terracotta offering vase are analogous to the ones depicted on many artefacts of Sumerian art, such as the Plaque of Ur-Nanše or the Relief representing a libation to a god from archaic Ur (Fig. 23). Among the truly exceptional artefacts found on the

---

[161] Comparable terracotta offering containers have been uncovered e.g. in the White Temple complex of Umm al-Aqarib (probably ancient Gišša), H. Almamori pers. comm.

plaza's earthen floor were a votive bronze figurine or amulet of a palmiped (duck) featuring inlaid eyes of shell, perhaps dedicated to Nanše, goddess associated with water, marshlands, and aquatic birds,[162] and a fragment of a Protodynastic inscribed calcite vase dedicated to Ningirsu.

In sum the exploration of Area A provided important insights into both the spatial organization of the sacred precinct of Girsu and the rituals related to the central great cult of the city-state in the Early Dynastic period. The general layout of the Uruku composed of peripheral temples probably standing on high terraces or platforms dedicated to the chief gods of the Lagaš pantheon, like the oval-complex of the tutelary deity Ningirsu, revolved around a large ceremonial square (or temenos) established below and featuring all the installations and other structures necessary for the state's prime religious ceremonies. The presence of a considerable quantity of terracotta cups, bowls, and several cultic spouted jars, a large libation vessel, votive artefacts, as well as burnt floors and of course a ritual deposit including hundreds of broken goblets and bones strongly connects the partially exposed plaza to the area where according to the Presargonic cuneiform tablets religious festivals took place and where the population of Girsu gathered to feast and honor their gods.

---

[162] H. Almamori pers. comm.

Chapter Four

Demarcated by the Gods. Sumerian Rites and the Lagaš-Umma Border Conflict

The god Enlil, king of the lands, father of the gods, by his authoritative command, demarcated the border between the gods Ningirsu and Šara.[163]

The Sumerian Concept of Sacred Territoriality

According to the theocratic ideology or dogma, Early Dynastic Sumer, since time-immemorial, was held as a coherent political-religious system with the existence of divinely sanctioned borders between rival city-states, such as Uruk, Ur-Eridu, and of course Girsu-Lagaš and Umma-Zabalam.[164] That the Sumerian chief cities and the seats of tutelary deities formed single entities, which is already implicit in the Uruk protohistorical period on the basis of the Archaic City List, was repeatedly expressed in the large corpus of royal inscriptions of Presargonic times. In Ancient Sumer like in Classical Greece territorial policy and cultic topography were therefore strongly interconnected.[165]

The fact that one of the principal aims of the propagandistic inscriptions was to seek a form of equilibrium of power relations and territorial claims between contending city-states may explain why the delimitation of these cities' areas of influence was assigned to the patron-gods and, thus, considered a divine prerogative. Hence Girsu's official inscriptions seek to recall the mythical past to locate the original frontier with Umma and make it inviolable. Such a conception is clearly linked to the well-known cosmological narratives and chronicles of which unfortunately only tenuous information is preserved in the Protodynastic epigraphical records. Yet late Sumerian literary materials of Old Babylonian times, like the already-cited myth Enki and the world order reflect the ordering of sacred spaces by the gods and the attribution of a destiny to the cities and their territories by the gods.[166]

Of course the religious consecration of cities, and thus, their countryside to chief deities of the Sumerian pantheon, is also attested in Presargonic times.[167] Since each center of power possessed its own tutelary deity, inter-state conflicts had clear corollaries in the divine sphere, any conquest or defeat constituting thereby an important change in a preset order. The En-metena royal inscription prologue, here emphasized in the epigraph, found on varying types of artefacts, such as a clay cone, a cylinder, and

---
[163] Cf. Frayne, D. 2008, p. 195, En-metena E1.9.5.1.
[164] Cf. Steinkeller, P. 1992, p. 725.
[165] Cf. Selz, G. 1995, p. 294-304; Rosengarten, Y. 1960. See Polignac, de F. 1995 on ancient Greece.
[166] Cf. Bottéro, J. & Kramer, S. 1989, p. 165-188.
[167] Cf. Lecompte, C. forthcoming.

fragments of clay vessels, explicitly referring to the demarcation of the city-states of Girsu-Lagaš and Umma-Zabalam, demonstrates this fact perfectly.[168] Enlil, the principal god of the Sumerian pantheon, patron-god of Nippur and 'occupying the position of the paterfamilias' defined the territorial space of both lesser gods: Ningirsu like Šara received their own land, cult-space, and were assigned their own fiefdom. Early territorial formation in Mesopotamia reflected therefore a complex theological construct that may not be assimilated to any state's particular political logic.

Another implication of the Sumerian concept of religious territorial fragmentation is reflected in the well-known records of Protodynastic conflicts such as the so-called Lagaš-Umma border dispute: based on the En-metena official inscription, the sacrilegious attempt of Uš ruler of Umma to invade Girsu and march on the Eden district of Lagaš was repelled by the patron-god Ningirsu in person, despite the fact that in reality this specific encounter corresponded of course to the phalanx battle led by E-anatum (super-champion of Ningirsu) depicted on the Stele of the Vultures. Yet the earthly intervention of Ningirsu appears to be directed against Umma as a geographical and spatial entity: 'The god Ningirsu, warrior of the god Enlil, at his just command, did battle with Umma'.[169] Assimilation between divinity and territory/city (i.e., Šara interchangeable with Umma, Ningirsu with Girsu or Lagaš) perhaps may be reflected in the capability of earthly lords to offend the tutelary gods by transgressing the spatial symbolic boundaries.

A royal inscription of Urukagina, the last ruler of Lagaš I, preserved on a clay tablet relating an attack against Girsu-Lagaš by Lugal-zagesi records in detail the so-called impious chain of violent devastations by the ruler of Umma (and Uruk) in Lagaš and its countryside, including many sanctuaries and nonurban shrines situated at the frontier: '(Lugal-za$_3$-ge-si) has (therefore) committed a sin against the god Ningirsu'.[170] Any infringement against a territorial space held as a religious patrimony tantamount to offend the divinity itself. However, one may wonder what part of rhetoric lay in the particular phraseology utilized by Urukagina if one considers that his predecessors (E-anatum, En-metena, cf. below) most likely altered to their benefit the course of the frontier that had been nonetheless decided by Enlil.

Contextualizing the Lagaš-Umma Border Conflict

The clash between the city-states of Girsu-Lagaš and Umma (or Gišša)-Zabalam definitely represents the first and best documented historiographic account of ongoing feuds between preeminent powers of the Early Dynastic period over agricultural lands and water rights.[171] Moreover according to J. Cooper it represents

---

[168] Cf. Frayne, D. 2008, p. 195, En-metena E1.9.5.1.
[169] En-metena E1.9.5.1 (Frayne, D. 2008, p. 195).
[170] URU-KA-gina E1.9.9.5 (p. 279).
[171] Cf. Pettinato, G. 1970-71, p. 281-320; Cooper, J. 1983; Steiner, G. 1986, p. 219-300; Almamori, H. 2014, p. 1-36;

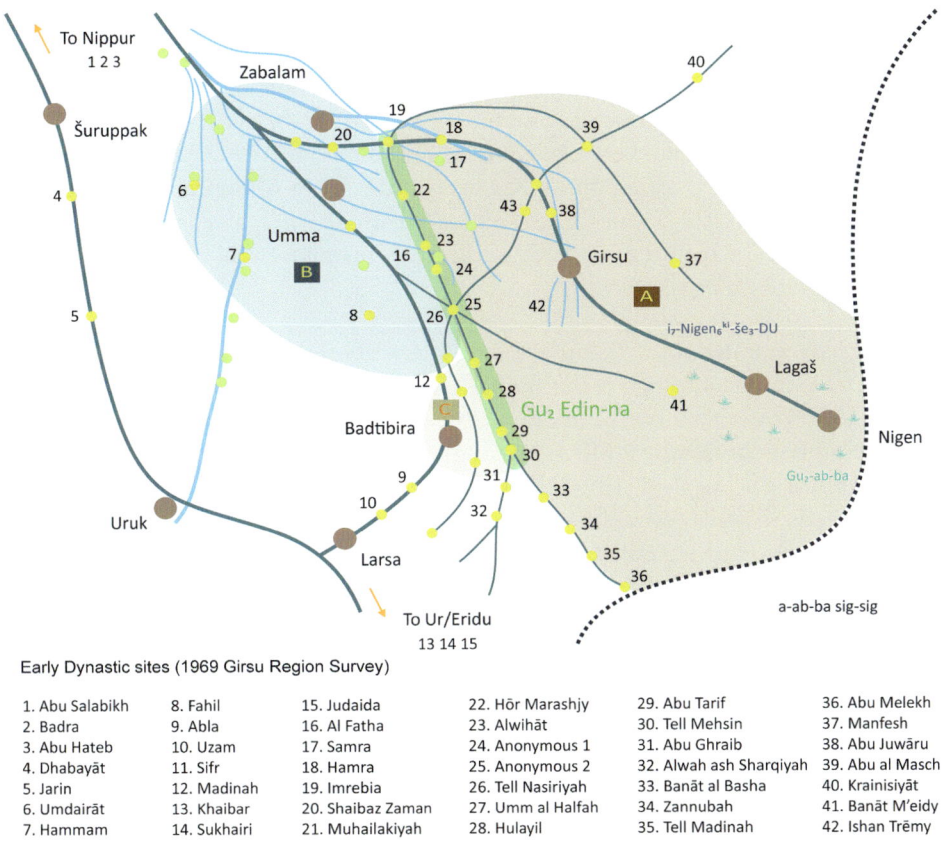

FIG. 24: THE EARLY DYNASTIC SUMERIAN ALLUVIUM FEATURING THE GU'EDENA FRONTIER BETWEEN (A) THE TERRITORIAL SPACE OF THE GIRSU-LAGAŠ CITY-STATE, (B) THE UMMA-ZABALAM CITY-STATE, (C) THE PORTION OF LAND AROUND BADTIBIRA ANNEXED BY EN-METENA (BASE MAP AFTER JACOBSEN, T., 1969, P. 109, AND ADAMS, R. 2008, P. 7)

the precursor of the 'theological rationale' of all later Babylonian imperialism, i.e., 'making war in the name of a god for territory claimed by a god or given to the warring ruler by a god'.[172]

As already suggested, in the course of the 3rd Millennium, the Land of Sumer developed a complex landscape of largely independent multiform city-states that contiguously bordered each other to form a 'closed political system' (Fig. 24).[173] This led to the constellation of fluctuating poliad alliances of varying morphologies, such

---

Selz, G. 2015, p. 387-404. For H. Almamori Gišša (present-day Umm al-Aqarib) represented the real metropolis of the GIŠ.KUŠU₂.KI city-state in Early Dynastic times not Umma (Jokha) considered to be then a lesser settlement (cf. p. 1-11).
[172] Cf. Cooper, J. 1983, p. 11.
[173] Cf. Steinkeller, P. 1992, p. 725.

as the so-called Kiengir league held as an amphictyony and led in the celestial sphere by the supreme-god Enlil of Nippur. The league also known as the Hexapolis, probably created in the ED IIIa period, the so-called Fāra epoch (ca. 2650 BC), included Šuruppak, Umma, Uruk, Nippur, Lagaš, and Adab, and either had ties with the megapolis of Kiš, then very likely the hegemonic power, or even lay completely under its rule. That the kingdom of Kiš exercised a form of supremacy over both Lagaš and Umma in ED II times (and perhaps as early as ED I) and greater Babylonia except Ur appears manifest in later dedicatory inscription of Girsu pertaining precisely to the border conflict.[174]

If as already pointed out, fixing the boundary represented a divinely privilege granted to Enlil, according to the Sumerian historical tradition, in the terrestrial sphere the god's decision had been originally carried out by his first or at least earliest known earthly holy nominee Me-salim king (lugal) of Kiš (contemporary and very likely overlord of Lugal-ša$_3$-ENGUR ruler (ensi$_2$) of Lagaš): 'At the place where Me-salim had erected a (boundary) monument (…)'[175]; 'Me-salim, king of Kiš at the command of the god Ištaran stretched the measuring rope on the field and erected a (boundary) monument there'.[176] The symbolic landmark of Me-salim apparently sanctioned the primordial border between Lagaš and Umma on the basis of the expression na-ru$_2$ which literally equates to the erection of a stone, therefore a stele, as attested in a royal inscription of Gišša-kidu of Umma.[177]

But in the aftermath of the probable weakening of the power of Kiš and of its sphere of influence and arbitrator role in the early ED III period (ca. 2650-2500 BC), the old alliance of the Hexapolis also presumably started to crack, leading precisely to the end of the Pax Sumerica under its aegis and to the regional 150 years' Lagaš-Umma border conflict (ca. 2500-2350 BC). From probably the reign of E-anatum of Lagaš (or perhaps his predecessor A-kurgal) to that of Lugal-zagesi of Umma (and Uruk) the bordering rival city-states battled, thus, fiercely and endlessly over contested tracts of rich irrigated lands on their common frontier known as the Gu'edena ('the edge of the plains').

Although the founder of the First Dynasty of Lagaš Ur-Nanše clearly engaged in bellicose operations against Umma (and Ur) on the basis of a royal inscription commemorating inter alia the construction of the Bagara temple of Ningirsu at Lagaš and stating that 'Ur-Nanše defeated and [captured] the leader of Ur (…) the leader of Umma'[178], it appears that the historical narrative of the Gu'edena dispute really started, according to J. Cooper, during E-anatum's reign: 'the border conflict as a leitmotif in the historical records of Lagaš and the various topoi that accompany

---

[174] Cf. Steinkeller, P. 2013, p. 131-157; Frayne, D. 2009.
[175] E-anatum E1.9.3.3 (Frayne, D. 2008, p. 143).
[176] En-metena E1.9.5.1 (p. 195).
[177] Gišša-kidu E1.12.6.2 (p. 373).
[178] Ur-Nanše E1.9.1.6b (p. 92).

it have their origin in the royal inscriptions of E-anatum'.[179] Yet according to the latter and also En-metena's official historiography, the feud originated in the time of A-kurgal of Lagaš because Umma's phalanx invaded the territory belonging to Ningirsu: 'Uš, ensi$_2$ of Umma, acted arrogantly; he ripped out (or smashed) that (Me-salim's) monument and marched on the Eden district of Lagaš'.[180]

Seeking probably to support from the start their supposed rightful claims, rulers of Lagaš invoked the arbitrator role of the archetypal ancestral persona of Me-salim (furthermore the representative of the god Enlil) in the delineation of both archaic states, as clearly evidenced by the En-metena royal inscription:

> E-anatum, ruler of Lagaš, uncle of En-metena, ruler of Lagaš, demarcated the border with En-akale, ruler of Umma. (…) He inscribed (and erected) monuments at that (boundary) dike and restored the monument of Me-salim, but did not cross into the Eden (district) of Umma.[181]

Yet this passage partly echoes the account of E-anatum in the Stele of the Vultures (Fig. 25): 'E-anatum, the man of just commands, measured off the boundary [from Umma], left (some land) under the control of Umma and erected a monument on that spot'.[182] The demarcation of the border occurred this time round without the intervention of an arbitrator because the ruler of Lagaš actually claimed to return to the prior situation sanctioned by Me-salim, i.e., before the conflict.

But the significance of supra-arbitration authorities (royal or godly) remains in fact uncertain and somewhat ambiguous: if indeed the metropolis of Kiš dominated the political scene in the ED II period, the king's intervention might merely better reflect the territorial policy of the principal Mesopotamian power of the time facing neighboring antagonistic client states. Yet E-anatum of Lagaš boasting later of having defeated among other powers like Elam, Ur, Uruk, Umma, Akšak, and Mari, the former super-power Kiš, which by then had completely lost its monopoly over the amphictyony, and, moreover, of having received from 'the goddess Inanna the kingship of Kiš in addition to the rulership of Lagaš',[183] the new geopolitical situation may not have lent itself anymore to the intercession of a former hegemonic authority. Rather the particular political development in the early ED III period may better explain why the ruler of Lagaš actually imposed new boundaries, even if it meant voluntarily displacing the milestones of Me-salim that he claimed to (carefully) restore.

The real ambition of E-anatum – not only to recover the part of the Ningirsu's Gu'edena fallen under the yoke of the god Šara (in the reign of A-kurgal) but to

---

[179] Cf. Cooper, J. 1983, p. 24.
[180] En-metena E1.9.5.1 (p. 195).
[181] En-metena E1.9.5.1 (p. 196).
[182] E-anatum E1.9.3.1 (p. 131).
[183] E-anatum E1.9.3.5 (p. 148).

annex new lands beyond the Umma border – was later amplified by En-metena who conquered Badtibira and established a form of 'brotherhood' (treaty) with Lugal-kineš-dudu of Uruk:

> En-metena, ruler of Lagaš, nominee of the god Ningirsu, at the just command of the god Enlil (…) constructed the (boundary) dike from the Tigris River to the Nin canal. He built the foundations of the Namninda-kigara for the god Ningirsu out of stone (…).[184]

Because the epigraphical sources pertaining to the Lagaš-Umma border dispute found on varying types of artefacts, including the Stele of the Vultures, Ur-Nanše's stone slab, E-anatum's boulders and clay pottery fragments, En-anatum I clay tablet, En-metena's clay cone and terracotta receptacles, Urukagina's clay disk, fragment of clay cylinder, and tablet,[185] have been nearly exclusively revealed at Tello/Girsu and Hiba/Lagaš and are consequently biased in favor of Lagaš's rightful claims, it appears rather problematic to impartially reconstruct the entire conflict and to catalog Umma's counter-claims.

Only a dedicatory inscription of Gišša-kidu of Umma found on a pottery fragment, a stone deposit tablet, and a limestone cone of unfortunately unknown provenience relates to the fixing of the so-called 'boundary of Šara' and presents Umma's interpretation of the conflict that interestingly mirrored the E-anatum and En-metena royal inscriptions.[186] After having recorded the ruler's epithets, the inscription recounted that the ruler established the boundary of Umma restoring the old markers, then referred to the frontier thoroughly (according to the monument of the god Šara), ending with a magical-curse formulae against anyone trespassing the boundary: 'Gišša-kidu, shepherd beloved of the god Šara (…) constructed (the boundary's) dyke, erected its monument, made its levee preeminent, and restored its (boundary) monuments (…)'.[187] To be sure both rival city-states appear, thus, to have rightful pretensions to the bordering rich agrarian lands.[188]

Yet for Lagaš's rulers, from perhaps E-anatum to Urukagina, their principal claims have continuously been precisely the Gu'edena, the so-called 'Ningirsu's beloved field'. The sovereigns of Girsu-Lagaš may accept nevertheless that their marcher territory belonging to their patron-god be occupied and partly cultivated by the forces (conscripts or laborers) of its neighboring tutelary god if naturally Umma agreed to pay interest-bearing loans and grain-rents, and to properly use the irrigation network (i.e., the boundary-channels and canals):

---

[184] En-metena E1.9.5.1 (p. 198).
[185] Cf. Cooper, J. 1983, p. 12-17.
[186] Cf. Almamori, H. 2014, p. 1-37.
[187] Gišša-kidu E1.12.6.2 (p. 373).
[188] Cf. Pettinato, G. 1970-71, p. 281-320.

'The leader of Umma swore to E-anatum: by the life of the god Enlil, king of heaven and earth! I may exploit the field of the god Ningirsu as a(n interest-bearing) loan';[189] '(…) Umma could exploit 1 gur (5184 hl.) of the barley of the goddess Nanše and the barley of the god Ningirsu as an (interest-)bearing loan'.[190]

Hence, according to J. Cooper, the Girsu-Lagaš city-state developed throughout the entire conflict a rather pragmatic and somewhat resourceful territorial policy against Umma-Zabalam based on a crafty theoretical construct: 'when Lagaš was strong, it might turn theory into fact and collect tribute from Umma (e.g., during the reigns of Ur-Nanše, perhaps also before Ur-Nanše, E-anatum, En-metena); when after a period of weakness (e.g., the reigns of A-kurgal, En-anatum I), Lagaš sought to regain part of the disputed territory from Umma, there was always a ready excuse to send ultimatums and finally resort to arms: Umma had failed to pay the requisite duties, or had exceeded its allotted acreage and transgressed the boundary'.[191]

FIG. 25: STELE OF THE VULTURES.
HISTORICAL SIDE PORTRAYING THE RULER E-ANATUM LEADING A PHALANX
(SARZEC E. DE & HEUZEY, L. 1884-1912, PL. 3-BIS)

---
[189] E-anatum E1.9.3.1 (p. 133).
[190] En-metena E1.9.5.1 (p. 196).
[191] Cf. Cooper, J. 1983, p. 23.

Characterizing the Presargonic Gu'edena frontier

If the French-led explorations of Tello/Girsu between 1877 and 1933 and the catastrophic large-scale lootings produced a richness of inscribed artefacts depicting the Lagaš-Umma border conflict, very few researches are in fact devoted to the geographical setting of the Sumerian Early Dynastic frontier. Careful re-assessment of these epigraphic records, the royal inscriptions and the bureaucratic tablets, in light of re-examination of the archaeological regional surveys of Babylonia by space imagery, led to reconstruct the general layout or anatomy of the Gu'edena border in Presargonic times.

Although philological problems may hinder the comprehension of Lagaš I textual sources it appears rather clear that the Sumerian logogram ki-sur-ra, literally designating 'demarcated land', refers to a well-defined coherent space that may be equivalent to both antique and modern concepts of the territory, precisely because it is determined by a boundary.[192] The compound verb ki-sur that denotes the act of circumscribing a territorial space in the archival corpus of Presargonic Girsu occurred at least twice in the En-metena royal inscription, first about the demarcation of the frontier by the god Enlil, then by the ruler.[193]

Hence the primary meaning of ki-sur-ra as border may be derived from the epigraphic occurrences, as explicitly evidenced in the En-anatum I royal inscription from Hiba/Lagaš pertaining to a particular dyke/channel (Sumerian e(g_2)-ki-sur-ra) designed to separate Lagaš and Umma's respective territories, and that Ur-lumma, the leader of Umma, transgressed:

> Ur-LUM-ma, ruler of (Umma), [hired] [(mercenaries from) the foreign lands] and transgressed the boundary-channel of the god Ningirsu (and said): '(the town) Antasurra ('Northern (?) Boundary') is mine! I shall exploit (its) *prebends*!'[194]

That the term ki-sur-ra equates to the Sumerian concept of frontier also appears in the Stele of the Vultures, i.e., during E-anatum's rather elaborate God-given triumph celebration, in the repeated oaths sworn by the ruler of Umma to the principal gods of the Sumerian pantheon Enlil, Niñursag̃, Enki, Sin, Utu, and Ninki:

> Forever and evermore, I shall not transgress the territory of the god Ningirsu! I shall not shift the course of its irrigation channels and canals! I shall not rip out its monuments! Whenever I do transgress, may the great battle net of Enlil, king of heaven and earth, by which I have sworn, descend upon Umma![195]

---

[192] C. Lecompte, pers. comm.
[193] En-metena E1.9.5.1 (p. 195).
[194] En-anatum I E1.9.4.2 (p. 172).
[195] E-anatum E1.9.3.1 (p. 133).

Presargonic royal inscriptions and the agro-managerial records from the Lagaš queen's manorial household revealed varying multifunction border features and the organization of the Gu'edena. On the basis of En-metena's inscription, E-anatum of Lagaš first established by royal command a ca. 1300 meter-wide buffer zone between the territorial spaces of Ningirsu and Šara:

> (E-anatum led off the (boundary) channel from the Nun canal to the Gu'edena district, leaving a 215 nindan (1290 m) (strip) of Ningirsu's land under the control of Umma and establishing a no-man's land there.[196]

The Gu'edena also appears to be characterized by artificial embankments (Sumerian im-dub-ba) clearly demarcating the frontier, such as the so-called im-dub-ba-^{d}Nin-ĝir$_2$-su levee.[197] Many of these large-scale earthworks including the latter probably featured apotropaic steles and were ritually sanctioned by shrines dedicated to important deities which ensured so to speak their symbolic stability: 'On the boundary-levee of the god Ningirsu (called) Namnun-kiĝara, (E-anatum) built a chapel of the god Enlil, a chapel of the goddess Ninḫursaĝ, a chapel of the god Ningirsu, and a chapel of the god Utu'.[198] Clearly these deities correspond to the principal gods of the Sumerian pantheon, the 'Eidgottheiten' according to G. Steiner,[199] including the Lord of Girsu, and by being worshipped in these border chapels may have theoretically provided a magical protection at the frontier.

Other large-scale hydraulic features accompanied the spatial composition and structural layout of the Lagaš-Umma border as evidenced by the existence of important workloads probably carried out by laborers or conscripts on some boundary canals and dikes (Sumerian eg$_2$). So-called eg$_2$ ki-sur-ra dikes are indeed attested in the Presargonic epigraphic records, including those belonging to the state of Lagaš's principal gods, Ningirsu and Nanše. On the basis of En-metena's propagandist historiography, the ruler of Umma Il arrogantly laid claim to both of these hydraulic structures: 'Il$_2$, ruler of Umma, the field thief, speaking hostilely, said: the boundary dike of the god Ningirsu and the boundary dike of the goddess Nanše are mine!'[200] That ruler, but also his predecessor Ur-lumma, sought to divert irrigation water from these dikes, which for a downstream bordering city-state clearly had to be seen as yet another casus belli: 'Ur-LUM-ma ruler of Umma diverted water from the boundary dike of the god Ningirsu and the boundary dike of the goddess Nanše'.[201]

The complex frontier network of canalization and border waterways, either water-supply installations or water-transport features, both probably designated by eg$_2$ ki-

---

[196] En-metena E1.9.5.1 (p. 196).
[197] En-metena E1.9.5.1 (p. 196); Gišša-kidu E1.12.6.2 (p. 373).
[198] En-metena E1.9.5.1 (p. 196).
[199] Cf. Steiner, G. 1986, p. 230.
[200] En-metena E1.9.5.1 (p. 198).
[201] En-metena E1.9.5.1 (p. 196).

sur-ra, also appears to be connected to the im-dub-ba earthen levees on the basis of a passage of En-metena's royal inscription recounting the latter episode. In the part of the Gu'edena held by Girsu, the eg$_2$ ki-sur-ra frontier watercourses and dykes may have been truly fundamental elements of the entire irrigation system of the rich agricultural border area. Perhaps that may explain why the ruler En-metena, after the irrigation water dispute incident against Umma, ordered the digging of another frontier dyke, 'the exalted boundary dike which the god Enlil demarcated for the god Ningirsu',[202] which according to G. Steiner duplicated the eg$_2$ dike of Ningirsu.[203] Another hydraulic border feature merely labeled eg$_2$ ki-sur-ra also occurred in the queen of Lagaš's archives dating to the reign of Lugal-Anda that referred apparently to a sacrifice at this particular location but without specifying the reason.[204] The eg$_2$ ki-sur-ra may also have been an open-area place of worship connected to a particular natural-symbolic element.

That the Gu'edena may have been besides its political-religious aspect a rich agrarian estate seems proven by the presence at the frontier of large-scale fields and agricultural lands in connection with boundary channels like the a-ša$_3$-GAN$_2$-ki-sur-ra where according to the inscribed brick of En-metena, the ruler boasted of a having erected a stele after the digging of the new eg$_2$-maḫ ki-sur-ra ^{d}En-lil$_2$-le ^{d}Nin-g̃ir$_2$-su-ra sur-ra.[205] Another indicator may also be the presence of rural granaries or storehouses (Sumerian g̃anun) and probable frontier hamlets (or farms perhaps comparable to villae rusticae) that as already suggested merely appear in the Presargonic tablets in nonurban context as e$_2$ settlements with assigned agricultural functions, and which to some extent might have been equivalent to the e$_2$-duru$_5$ of the Ur III period.[206] Several of these e$_2$ nonurban localities (like e$_2$-bar-ti-ra-aš$_2$, e$_2$-en-na, e$_2$-DU$_6$-me-kul-aba$_4$^{ki}-ta) very likely dotted not only the Girsu-Lagaš hinterlands but also the Gu'edena border area.

Fortification features formed an integral part of the Lagaš-Umma border's setting although their attestation from cuneiform tablets and inscribed artefacts appears rather scarce. If the Sumerogram bad$_3$ referenced to an Early Dynastic city (like bad$_3$ Lagaš^{ki}, bad$_3$ G̃ir$_2$-su^{ki})[207] ordinarily equates to an enceinte, it may also designate as already stated in Presargonic epigraphic sources a nonurban defended structure of varying morphology (a fortified farm, rural watchtower, border outpost), very comparable to the an-za-gar$_3$ of the Umma province's archive of Ur III times.[208] Lagaš I textual sources have thus revealed the presence throughout the territory of

---

[202] En-metena E1.9.5.2 (p. 200).
[203] Cf. Steiner, G. 1986, p. 235.
[204] C. Lecompte, pers. comm.
[205] En-metena E1.9.5.2 (p. 200).
[206] Cf. Lecompte, C. 2015, p. 211-246.
[207] Ur-Nanše E1.9.1.6b (p. 91); URU-KA-gina E1.9.9.1 (p. 259).
[208] Cf. Stenkeller, P. 2007, p.185-211; Lecompte, C. 2015, p. 211-246.

the city-state including the Gu'edena of these bad_3 independent fortification features defended by a special garrisoned force of gatekeepers (Sumerian i_3-du_8 bad_3).[209]

Many of the bad_3 rural strongholds either connected to fields (Sumerian GAN_2) and agricultural lands or to eg_2 dikes and pa_5 waterways may have been located at strategic areas of the Girsu countryside, and other bad_3 keeps associated to stocks of goods may have operated as large-scale storehouses or fortified granaries. A royal inscription of En-metena found on a boulder of unknown provenience celebrated the construction by the saĝĝa Dudu of the forefront bad_3 fortress of the Lagaš/Umma border: 'Dudu, the temple administrator of the god Ningirsu, built a fortress along the Sala (canal), in the Gu'edena district and named it 'Building that Surveys the Plain'.[210] Probably corresponding to the toponym e_2-igi-il_2 edin-na, the bad_3 da-sal_4 Gu_2-edin-na clearly appears to have been the principal border fortress, i.e., the spearhead of the frontier's fortification network.

Yet that the Gu'edena ('Ningirsu's beloved field') primarily was considered by Presargonic Girsu as a holy territorial space has already been posited both theoretically on the basis of the state official ideology and cosmological construct, and concretely by the presence of marcher shrines dedicated to the principal Sumerian gods facing the territory of Umma and its patron-god Šara. That the important cult-center of Girsu's patron-god Antasura lay in the Gu'edena and especially in the neighborhood of the eponymous city-state capital Umma appears far from trivial: if according to the Lagaš state's political phraseology the disputed Gu'edena clearly was held as 'Ningirsu's beloved field', Antasurra, considered the god's principal rural sanctuary, a place subject to cultic offerings from an epoch prior to the reign of Ur-Nanše, whence the ruler E-anatum defeated the combined forces of Kiš, Akšak, and Mari, to which Ur-lumma of Umma repeatedly laid claim, and among the first frontier temples sacked by Lugal-zagesi, also might very likely have been a symbol of the Lagaš-Umma border.[211]

The Gu'edena probably reached a surface area of ca. 60 to 80 square-kilometers in Presargonic times.[212] Except for a minor portion of land roughly situated between Zabalam (modern Ibzaykh) and Muhalliqiya (perhaps ancient Apišal), and a small area located around present-day Nasiriya at the Lagaš-Umma frontier – though both regions peculiarly appear only on the map of the Akkadian–Old Babylonian settlements and watercourses, not on the Early Dynastic one – almost the entire landscape of the Girsu-Lagaš city-state (and the principal part of the Gu'edena) lay outside the boundaries of the Uruk regional survey carried out by R. Adams and H. Nissen in 1967, updated since using satellite imagery.[213]

---

[209] Cf. Lecompte, C. forthcoming.
[210] En-metena E1.9.5.27 (p. 232).
[211] Cf. Cooper, J. 1983, p. 32.
[212] Cf. Pettinato, G. 1970-71, p. 306 (41 km² in the Ur III period).
[213] Cf. Adams, R. & Nissen, H. 1972; Adams, R. 2008, p. 7.

Only the Girsu surface prospection conducted by T. Jacobsen, and to some extent the pioneering reconnaissance of G. Cros in the near periphery of Tello as early as 1903,[214] shed light on the spatial organization of the Presargonic border: of the 40 Early Dynastic archaeological sites surveyed in 1969 not less than 20 were located in the Gu'edena area and in the Badtibira neighborhood.[215] A few of these Protodynastic sites as well as several waterways have been connected by T. Jacobsen to well-known Presargonic toponyms: Imrebi'a (19)/Antasurra, Nasiriya (26)/part of the Namnun-kigara (Tigris feeder), perhaps Anonymous 1 (24)/one of the border chapels (?) or nearby the Ugiga-field where En-anatum I of Lagaš supposedly repulsed Umma's chariotry:

> En-anatum, ruler of Lagaš, fought with (Ur-LUM-ma) in the Ugiga-field, the field of the god Ningirsu. En-metena, beloved son of En-anatum, deafeted him. Ur-LUM-ma escaped, but was killed in Umma itself. His asses – there were 60 teams(?) of them – he abandoned on the bank of LUM-ma-ğirnunta canal, and left the bones of their personnel strewn over the Eden district.[216]

Of course the precise geographical localizations of these border features (canals, dykes, shrines) attested in the Lagaš I cuneiform tablets and royal inscriptions are extremely difficult or impossible to determine before renewed large-scale ground exploration becomes possible revealing in situ inscribed diagnostic artefacts. Yet it appears very likely that the eg_2 ki-sur-ra boundary canal-dike of Ningirsu and the eg_2 ki-sur-ra boundary canal-dike of Nanše constituted contiguous reaches of a larger structure, maybe the eg_2-maḫ ki-sur-ra ^{d}En-lil$_2$-le ^{d}Nin-ğir$_2$-su-ra sur-ra,[217] demarcating the entire Lagaš-Umma frontier, the former from Imrebi'a (19)/Antasurra to perhaps Nasiriya (26), the latter from Nasiriya (26) to Mehsin (30) facing Badtibira.

The Rise of the Mesopotamian Imperial State

The dramatic apotheosis of the Lagaš-Umma 150 years' conflict parallels the rise of a new form of Babylonian imperialism, precursor to the hegemonic state of Akkad, embodied by the ruler Lugal-zagesi of Umma (and Uruk). The triumph of the latter's territorial policy of conquest (and unification) of Mesopotamia dialectically equates to the collapse of the balance of power or status-quo between neighboring Sumerian city-states. Despite its complex triad organization, the city-state of Girsu-Lagaš fell violently against a greater foe, a truly behemoth state unifying a new confederacy of metropolises (Uruk, Ur, Umma, Nippur) led by a charismatic omnipotent ruler. A dedicatory inscription found on stone artefacts from Nippur, thus, celebrated the new expansionist super-power by a well-known topos soon-to-be in all later Sargonic/Ur III propaganda:

---

[214] Cf. Cros, G. 1910, p. 19-20.
[215] Cf. Jacobsen, T. 1969, p. 103-109.
[216] En-metena E1.9.5.1 (p. 197).
[217] Contra Steiner, G. 1986, p. 235.

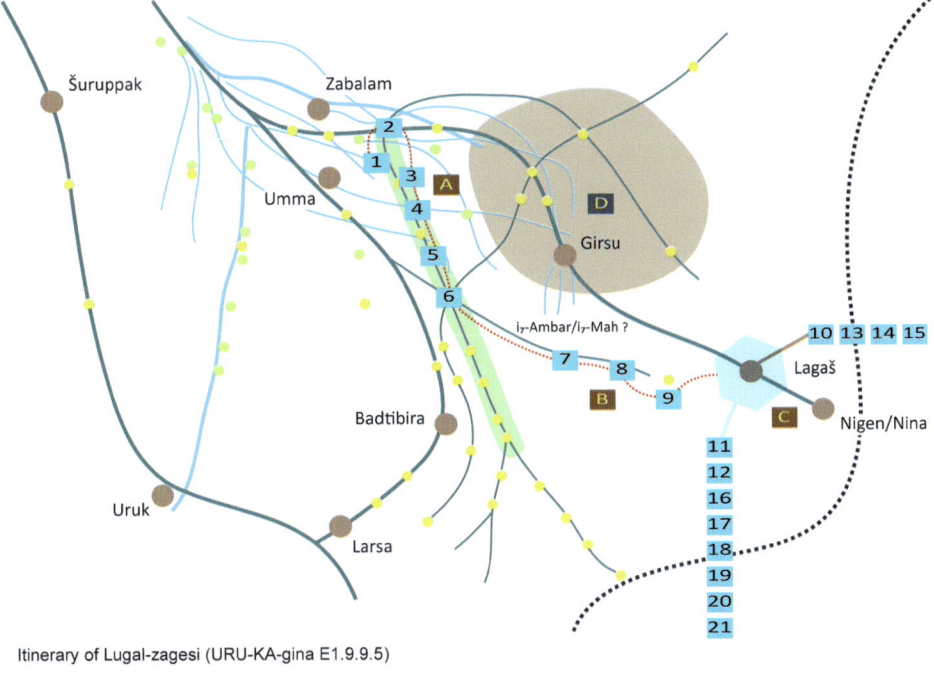

Itinerary of Lugal-zagesi (URU-KA-gina E1.9.9.5)

1. Eg₂ ki-sur(x)-ra (Marcher shrine)
2. An-ta-sur-ra (Sanctuary of Ningirsu)
3. Ti-ra-aš₂ᵏⁱ (Cult-place)
4. Abzu-banda₃-da (Chapel)
5. Para₁₀-ᵈEn-lil₂-la₂ (Chapel of Enlil)
6. Para₁₀-ᵈUtu (Chapel of Utu)
7. A-Huš (Walled sanctuary/town)
8. E₂-babbar₂ (Fortified cult-place/town)
9. Gi-gu₃-na-ᵈNin-mah-tir-ku₃-ga (Sanctuary)
10. Ba-gara₂ (Temple of Ningirsu in Lagaš)
11. Dug-ru (Large cult-center/town)
12. Abzu-e (Rural chapel)
13. E₂-ᵈGa₂-tum₃-du₁₀ (Temple of Gatumdug)
14. Ib-e₂-an-na-ᵈInanna (Temple of Inanna)
15. Ša₃-pa₃-da (Temple of Nanše)
16. HE-EN-DA (Rural reed shrine)
17. Ki-eš₃ᵏⁱ (Temple E₂-ᵈNin-dar)
18. Ki-nu-nirᵏⁱ (Temple E₂-ᵈDumu-zi-abzu)
19. Uru₁₁ᵏⁱ (Temple Lugal-Uru₁₁ᵏⁱ)
20. E₂-Engur-ra-ᵈNanše (Rural chapel)
21. Sag-ug₅ (Temple E₂-ᵈAma-geštin-na)

FIG. 26: RECONSTRUCTION OF THE LUGAL-ZAGESI CAMPAIGN AGAINST LAGAŠ BASED ON A PRESARGONIC ROYAL INSCRIPTION FEATURING THE THREE WAVES OF SACRILEGIOUS DESTRUCTIONS: (A) IN THE GU'EDENA, (B) DURING THE MARCH TO LAGAŠ, AND (C) IN THE CITY AND ITS SURROUNDINGS; (D) THE PROBABLE EXTENT OF URUKAGINA'S TERRITORY AFTER THE RAID.

> Enlil, king of the lands, gave to Lugal-zage-si the kingship of the land (…), from the Lower Sea, (along) the Tigris and Euphrates to the Upper Sea, he (Enlil) put their roads in good order for him. (…) Enlil permitted him no rival.[218]

The last campaign of Lugal-zagesi against Lagaš recorded on Urukagina's royal inscription that passed through the Gu'edena (but spared Girsu) has been schematically mapped (Fig. 26). The raid that deliberately (and systematically) ripped the border steles and targeted almost exclusively sanctuaries, temples, shrines devoted to the gods of the Girsu pantheon included three consecutive waves of destructions: (1) at the Lagaš-Umma border; (2) during the march between the frontier and the Lagaš neighborhood; (3) at the city of Lagaš and its near periphery.[219] As already

---

[218] Lugal-zage-si E1.14.20.1 (p. 436).
[219] URU-KA-gina E1.9.9.5 (p. 276-279).

mentioned, one of the first symbolic places beleaguered by Lugal-zagesi's phalanx in the Gu'edena was Antasurra (probably Imrebi'a (19), at the north-westernmost part of the city-state), Ningirsu's nonurban sanctuary. Many of the border chapels established by Lagaš I rulers along the eg$_2$ ki-sur-ra boundary canal-dike of Ningirsu (the Namnun-kiĝara), very likely between Imrebi'a (19) and Nasiriya (26), were also plundered or torched (abzu-banda$_3$-da, para$_{10}$-^{d}En-lil$_2$-la$_2$, para10-^{d}Utu).

The route to Lagaš (bypassing Girsu) followed by the Umma-Uruk campaigning army to be sure proves rather difficult to reconstruct but may have followed for purely logistical purposes the hypothetical archaic waterway proposed by T. Jacobsen running from northwest to southeast connecting Nasiriya (26) to Banāt M'eidy (41) nearby the bordering marshlands of Lagaš. The presupposed Early Dynastic watercourse may have been the i$_7$-Ambar/i$_7$-Mah of the Presargonic cuneiform tablets. Lugal-zagesi's inexorable warring party so depicted in Girsu's propaganda records razed important walled cult-places probably located along a large-scale water-transport feature, or at least northwest (or west) of Lagaš (A-huš, E$_2$-babbar$_2$, gi-gu$_3$-na-^{d}Nin-mah-tir-ku$_3$-ga).

Finally, Lugal-zagesi seized the metropolis of Lagaš, and perpetrated an unparalleled sacrilegious mayhem according to Girsu's historiographers, by thoroughly plundering the Bagara temple of Ningirsu (at the northwest of the city), the E$_2$-^{d}Ga$_2$-tum$_3$-du$_{10}$ (the shrine of Gatumdu, tutelary goddess of Lagaš), the Ib-e$_2$-an-na-^{d}Inanna (the Ibgal of Inanna, at the southwest of the city), and the Ša$_3$-pa$_3$-da temple of Nanše. Precious votive artefacts either in metal (bronze) or lapis lazuli were looted, the statuary shattered. And while part of Lugal-zagesi's troops set fire to Lagaš's urban sanctuaries, others ravaged the countryside, destroying secondary temples in neighboring towns (E$_2$-^{d}Nin-dar at Ki-eš$_3^{ki}$, E$_2$-^{d}Dumu-zi-abzu at Ki-nu-nir^{ki}, Lugal-Uru$_{11}^{ki}$ at Uru$_{11}^{ki}$), rural chapels (Abzu-e, E$_2$-engur-ra-^{d}Nanše), and torching Ningirsu's fields of barley.

After the Lugal-zagesi predatory conquest or rampage of the Gu'edena area and the entire southern part of the Lagaš state, the realm of Urukagina (henceforth only lugal G̃ir$_2$-su^{ki}) may have been restricted to the religious megapolis of Girsu and its near hinterlands. The Urukagina clay tablet represents the last known historical narrative (or epilogue) of the Lagaš-Umma border conflict, a precursor to the well-known literacy genre of the Ur III laments of Sumerian cities (Ur, Nippur, Eridu, Uruk). Because the ruler of Umma (and Uruk) according to the Lagaš phraseology utilized by Urukagina's royal scribes committed an irreparable blasphemous act against Ningirsu by trespassing the territory of the patron-deity, and razing temples, the people of Umma were cursed by the gods for eternity: 'May Nissaba, the god of Lugal-zage-si (…) make them bear this sin on their necks!'.[220]

---

[220] URU-KA-gina E1.9.9.5 (p. 279).

Conclusion: Morphogenesis of an Archaic City-State

Girsu, Iraq – once a radiant city whose 'splendor covered all the land', now almost forgotten engulfed in the providential floodplain of Mesopotamia. Scattered throughout the buried ruins votive artefacts dedicated to Ningirsu, Ba'u, Nanše are the lingering surface relics of the antique sacredness of Girsu, a city once shaped for the gods.

*

In a truly original study on the origins of the Greek city, the Hellenist F. de Polignac argued that religion – the central cult together with rites performed at the edge of the territory – played a crucial part in the formation of the ancient polis. 'In the bipolar view of the city (he wrote), the idea of a central point is not abolished but complemented by that of a median point. The two were linked through the axis of relations by means of which the city was elaborated and around which the secondary cults, whether of gods or of heroes, in the settlement or in its fringes, within the territory or on its boundaries, delineated and defined the functions of appropriation, delimitation, interconnection, and integration and affirmed the city's identity and sovereignty as a polis. Some of those concepts were coordinated and synthesized in the great sanctuary out in the territory, others in the great sanctuary in the heart of the town.'[221]

To be sure the schema of the nascent Greek city reconstructed by F. de Polignac cannot be generalized or applied indiscriminately to Southern Babylonia but only referred to as a revealing operative model. In Ancient Sumer the emergence or specifically the morphogenesis of the archaic city-state of Girsu-Lagaš probably also happened primarily through the mediation of religion. Yet the importance in particular of the peripheral pole, the 'median point', should hardly be overestimated. Although the Protodynastic border sanctuary of Antasura, the prime nonurban temple of Ningirsu and terminus of the state's paramount ritual procession, was the focus of ongoing disputes between Lagaš and Umma and therefore appear rather instrumental in the formation of territorial spheres of control, the 'central pole' located in the Uruku sanctum at the heart of the sacred city of Girsu, through the cult of the supreme tutelary god, remained the focal point around which the city-state crystalized.

Beyond of course its purely symbolic role, the Eninnu religious complex belonging to Ningirsu emerged at the twilight of protohistory as a locus of managerial activity as evidenced by the presence of the archaic tablets of the Fāra period or the *Figure aux plumes* containing probably the first sculpted depiction of the heroic war-god facing a sanctuary or apotropaic threshold and bearing a peculiar feathers' tiara, perhaps a symbol of Imdugud, the thunder-bird emblem of the god, or a reminiscence of the

---

[221] Cf. Polignac, F. de 1995 (1984), p. 154.

god's avatar or totem (Fig. 27). The archaic plaque included rather opaque recorded transactions involving real estate in connection with the temple, as well as a hymn to the god, which reflect therefore an inextricable relationship from the beginning linking the staging of a supernatural event with material production.

Girsu developed in the course of the Early Dynastic period into a proper megapolis consisting of multi-purpose spaces connected to a complex network of canalization and waterways: (1) an elevated sacred walled-precinct (mutatis mutandis, an acropolis)

FIG. 27: ARCHAIC BAS-RELIEF OF THE *FIGURE AUX PLUMES* RECORDING THE EARLIEST KNOWN OCCURRENCE OF THE SANCTUARY OF NINGIRSU (E_2-^{D}NIN-ĜIR$_2$-SU).

of large-scale symbolically charged cultic architecture revolving around a ceremonial square established below the religious complex of the patron deity standing on a rather elaborately prepared high terrace and consecrated platform enclosed by an oval-temenos; (2) a large-scale defended space of combined pre-planned religious areas (e.g., the peripheral temple of Nanše), secular political agro-managerial hubs – perhaps the so-called Mound of the Tablets – and presumably plebeian residential areas that probably grew organically; (3) an extramural district consisting of other domestic quarters and maybe storage facilities set along a mega-canal, the principal nexus serving the centers of the city-state; and (4) a suburban area of neighboring loose agglomerations or outlying open habitats, such as peripheral chapels, granaries, remote towers, and probably large farms.

The eidetic representation of the great urban cult center of Ningirsu composed of structurally interlocked symbolic features that reflect therefore a sacral hierarchy may be perceived as a Russian Doll (i.e., following the well-known Matryoshka paradigm): (1) the core sanctum sanctorum very likely being the shrine of Girsu ($Eš_3$-$\tilde{G}ir_2$-su interchangeable with E_2-^{d}Nin-$\tilde{G}ir_2$-su); (2) the shrine of Girsu encompassed in (or equal to) the temple of Ningirsu (E_2-ninnu); (3) the temple of Ningirsu situated within the sacred precinct (Iri-ku_3); (4) the holy precinct being part of Girsu ($\tilde{G}ir_2$-su^{ki}); and (5) the latter serving as the prime ceremonial center of the city-state.

The Girsu countryside, from the suburbs of the state's urban triad (Girsu, Lagaš, and Niğen) to the edge of the territory characterized by magical border steles, traversed by a landscape of anastomotic watercourses and marshes, developed organically throughout Presargonic times into a continuum of rural settlements of varying forms, such as villages, fortified storehouses, watchtowers, nonurban shrines, frontier sanctuaries. Pilgrimage rites in honor of the chief-gods of the Lagaš pantheon, Ningirsu, Ba'u, and Nanše, regularly repeated across the land guaranteed a sort of territorial unity at the symbolic level. Superimposed on a map the centrifugal ritual processions radiating from the Uruku sacred precinct and its ceremonial square at the heart of the temple area of Girsu and the border pilgrimage rituals at the edge of the territory delineate together the moving territorial space. In sum they appear as powerful structuring symbols for both the political formation and the social constitution of the city-state.

The Sumerian Rulers of the Early Dynastic Period

Period	Ur	Uruk	Girsu-Lagaš	Umma	Kiš
ED I		Gilgameš			Me-parasi ↓
					Aka ↓
ED II				Akinana ↑↓	Munus-adgal (?)
ED IIIa					Lugal-men (?)
					Lugal-utu
		Lumma			Me-nunsi
			Lugal-ša-engur		Me-salim
	Urpabilsağ ↑↓	Ursağpa-e (?)		Parasagnudi	
	Mesnunki-ağ			E-abzu	
ED IIIb			Ur-Nanše	Pabilgagaltuku	A-anzu (?)
	Aka-lamdu	Lugalnamniršum	A-kurgal	Uš	Enna-il
		Lugal-tarsi	E-anatum		Zuzu of Akšak
	Mes-kalamdu			En-akale	
	Mes-anepada		En-anatum I	Ur-lumma	
	A-anepada	Urzag-e	En-metena	Il	
	Lugal-kineš-dudu			Gišša-kidu	
			En-anatum II	Me-anedu	
	Lugal-kisalsi		En-entarzi	Ušurdu	
			Lugal-Anda	Eden	
	E-lili	Urni	Urukagina	U₂.u₂	
		Lugal-TAR		Lugal-zagesi	Enbi-eštar
	Enšakušana				Urzababa (?)
	Lugal-zagesi		Mes-zi	Mes-e	Sargon of Akkad
	Lu-Nanna	Girim-si	Kituš-i	EnnaLUM	

Bibliography

Adams, R. McC. 1966, *The Evolution of Urban Society. Early Mesopotamia and Prehispanic Mexico*, New Brunswick & London.

— 1981, *Heartland of Cities, Surveys of Ancient Settlement and Land Use on the Central Floodplain of the Euphrates*, Chicago & London.

— 2008, An Interdisciplinary Overview of a Mesopotamian City and its Hinterlands, *Cuneiform Digital Library Journal* 1, p. 1-23.

Adams, R. McC. & Nissen, H. J. 1972, *The Uruk Countryside, The Natural Setting of Urban Societies*, Chicago & London.

Almamori, H. 2014, Gišša (Umm al-Aqrib), Umma (Jokha) and Lagaš in the Early Dynastic III Period, *Al-Rāfidān* 35, p. 1-38.

Barrelet, M.-T. 1965, Une construction 'énigmatique' à Tello, *Iraq* 27, p. 100-118.

Bauer, J. 1971. Altsumerische Wirtschaftstexte aus Lagash, Rome

— 1998. Der vorsargonische Abschnitt der mesopotamischen Geschichte, *Mesopotamien: Späturuk-Zeit und Frühdynastische Zeit*, in Attinger P. and Wäffler M. (Ed.), p. 429-535

Bloch, M. 1983, *Les rois thaumaturges. Étude sur le caractère surnaturel attribué à la puissance royale, particulièrement en France et en Angleterre*, Paris.

Bottéro, J. 2001 (1998), *Religion in Ancient Mesopotamia*, Chicago & London.

Bottéro, J. & Kramer, S. 1989, *Lorsque les dieux faisaient l'homme. Mythologie mésopotamienne*, Paris.

Carroué, F. 1983, Les villes de l'État de Lagaš au 3ᵉ Millénaire, in *La ville dans le Proche-Orient Ancien*, Actes du Colloque de Cartigny 1979, Centre d'Etude du Proche-Orient Ancien (CEPOA), Université de Genève, Leuven p. 97-112.

— 1986, Le 'cours d'eau allant à NINA^ki', *Acta Sumerologica* 8, p. 13-57.

Cooper, J. 1983, *Reconstructing History from Ancient Inscriptions: The Lagaš-Umma Border Conflict*, Malibu.

Crawford, H. 1987, The Construction Inférieure at Tello. A reassessment, *Iraq* 49, p. 71-76.

Cros, G. (avec le concours de L. Heuzey et de F. Thureau-Dangin) 1910, *Nouvelles fouilles de Tello*, Paris.

Deimel, A. 1931, *Sumerische Tempelwirtschaft zur Zeit Urukaginas und seiner Vorgänger, Abschluss der Einzelstudien und Zusammenfassung der Hauptresultate*, Rome.

Edzard, D. 1997, *Gudea and His Dynasty*. Royal Inscriptions of Mesopotamia Early Periods 3/1, Toronto.

Diakonoff, I. 1974, *Structures of Society and State in Early Dynastic Sumer*, Malibu.

Falkenstein, A. 1966, *Die Inschriften Gudeas von Lagaš*, I. *Einleitung*. AnOr 30.

— 1974, *The Sumerian Temple City*, Malibu.

Forest, J.-D. 1996, *Mésopotamie. L'apparition de l'État*, Paris.

— 1999, *Les premiers temples de Mésopotamie* (4e et 3e millénaires), BAR International Series 765, Oxford.

Foster, B. 1981, A New Look at the Sumerian Temple State, in *Journal of Economy, Society and History of the Ancient Orient* 24, p. 225-241.

Frayne, D. 2008, *Presargonic Period* (2700-2350 BC). Royal Inscriptions of Mesopotamia Early Periods 1, Toronto.

— 2009, The Struggle for Hegemony in "Early Dynastic II" Sumer, *The Canadian Society for Mesopotamian Studies* 4, 37-76

Gelb, I. 1969, On the Alleged Temple and State Economies, in *Studi in onore di E. Volterra*, Rome, p. 137-154.

Gelb, I., Steinkeller, P., Whiting, R. 1991, *Earliest Land Tenure Systems in the Near East: Ancient Kudurrus*, Chicago.

Genouillac, H. de 1930a, La campagne du printemps 1929 à Tello, *Journal Asiatique* 217, p. 1-40.

— 1930b, Rapports sur les travaux de la mission de Tello (IIe campagne 1929-1930), *Revue d'Assyriologie* 27, p. 169-186.

Genouillac, H. de et al. 1934-36, *Fouilles de Telloh*, 1. Époques Présargoniques ; 2. Époques d'Ur IIIe Dynastie et de Larsa, Paris.

George, A. 1993, *House Most High. The Temples of Ancient Mesopotamia*, Winona Lake (Ind.).

Glassner, J.-J. 2000, Les petits États mésopotamiens à la fin du 4ème et au cours du 3ème millénaire, in *A Comparative Study of Thirty City-State Cultures*, Hansen M. (Ed.), Copenhagen, p. 35-53.

Heuzey, L. 1900, *Une villa royale chaldéenne vers l'an 4000 avant notre ère, d'après les levés et les notes de M. de Sarzec*, Paris.

Hocart, A. 1970 (1936), *Kings and Councillors. An Essay in the Comparative Anatomy of Human Society*, Chicago.

Huh, S. 2008, *Studien zur Region Lagaš: von der Ubaid bis zur altbabylonischen Zeit*, Münster.

Jacobsen, T. 1943, Primitive Democracy in Ancient Mesopotamia, in *Journal of Near Eastern Studies* 2, p. 159-172.

— 1957. Early Political development in Mesopotamia, *Zeitschrift für Assyriologie* 52, p. 91-140.

— 1960, The Waters of Ur, *Iraq* 22, p. 174-185.

— 1969, A Survey of Girsu (Telloh) Region, in *Sumer* 25, p. 103-109.

— 1976, *The Treasures of Darkness. A History of Mesopotamian Religion*, Yale.

Kramer, S. N. & Maier, J. 1989, *Myths of Enki, The Crafty God*, New York & Oxford.

Krebernik, M. 1998, Die Texte aus Fāra und Tell Abū Ṣalābīḫ, *Mesopotamien. Späturuk-Zeit und Frühdynastische Zeit*, P. Attinger and M. Wäfler (Ed.), Freiburg-Göttingen.

Lion, B. & Michel, C. (Ed.) 2009, *Histoire de déchiffrements. Les écritures du Proche-Orient à l'Égée*, Paris.

Lecompte, C. 2014, Review of Huh, S. 2014, *Orientalische Literaturzeitung* 109, 4-5, p. 1-4.

— 2015, Untersuchungen zu den Siedlungsstrukturen und den ländlichen Siedlungen in der FD-Zeit. Auf der Suche nach den verlorenen Dörfern in den altsumerischen Urkunden, *It's a Long Way to a Historiography of the Early Dynastic Period(s)*, R. Dittman and G. Selz (Ed.), p. 211-246.

— forthcoming. *Villes, villages et premiers États. Le territoire des cités sumériennes*, ISLET, Dresde.

Maekawa, K. 1973/74, The Development of E-MI in Lagash during Early Dynastic III, in *Mesopotamia* 8/9, p. 77-144.

Marchesi, G. & Marchetti, N. 2011, *Royal Statuary of Early Dynastic Mesopotamia*, Winona Lake (Ind).

Margueron, J.-C. 2005, Un pont enjambant un canal à Tello ?, *Syria* 82, p. 63-92.

Nissen, H. 1990 (1988), *The Early History of the Ancient Near East* (9000-2000 BC), Chicago & London.

Liverani, M. 1999, The Role of the Village in Shaping the Ancient Near Eastern Rural Landscape, in *Landscapes, Territories, Frontiers and Horizons in the Ancient Near East*, L. Milano et al. (Ed.), Padua, p. 37-47.

Parrot, A. 1932, Fouilles de Tello, campagne 1931-1932, *Revue d'Assyriologie* 29, p. 45-57.

— 1948, *Tello, Vingt campagnes de fouilles* (1877-1933), Paris.

Pemberton, W. et al. 1988, Canals and Bunds, Ancient and Modern, Irrigation and Cultivation in Mesopotamia, *Bulletin on Sumerian Agriculture* 4, Cambridge, p. 207-221.

Pettinato, G. 1970-71, Il conflitto tra Lagaš ed Umma per la 'Frontiera Divina' e la sua soluzione durante la terza dinastia di Ur, *Mesopotamia* 5-6, p. 281-320.

Pillet, M. 1958, Ernest de Sarzec, explorateur de Tello (1832-1901), *Comptes rendus des séances de l'Académie des Inscriptions et Belles-Lettres* 102/1, p. 52-62.

Pinches, T.G. 1912, Notices of Books, *Journal of the Royal Asiatic Society*, (New Series) 44 (3), p. 829–831.

Polignac, de F. 1995, *Cults, Territory, and the Origins of the Greek City-State*, Chicago.

Pomponio, F. and Visicatto, G. 1994. *Early Dynastic Administrative Tablets of* Šuruppak, Naples.

Pournelle, J. 2003, *Marshland of Cities: Deltaic Landscapes and the Evolution of Early Mesopotamian Civilization*. Ph.D. dissertation, University of California, San Diego.

— 2007, KLM to CORONA: A Bird's-Eye View of Cultural Ecology and Early Mesopotamian Urbanization, *Settlement and Society: Essays dedicated to Robert McCormick Adams*, E. Stone (Ed.), p. 29-62.

Rey, S. 2015, Il était une fois l'antique Girsu. Ou Tello et la redécouverte des Sumériens, in *Art&Fact*, Liège, p. 55-62.

Rey, S., Husain, F. & Lecompte, C. forthcoming, Tello/Girsu. Preliminary Report of the April 2015 Site Reconnaissance, *Sumer* (Baghdad).

Rey, S. & Lecompte, C. in press, Resurrecting Tello (Ancient Girsu): The Topographical Layout of an Early Dynastic Sumerian City, *New Agendas in Remote Sensing and Landscape Archaeology: Studies in Honor of Tony J. Wilkinson*, D. Lawrence, M. Altaweel and G. Philip (Ed.), Chicago.

Rosengarten, Y. 1960, *Le concept sumérien de consommation dans la vie économique et religieuse.* Étude linguistique et sociale d'après les textes présargoniques de Lagaš, Paris.

Sallaberger, W. & Schrakamp, I. (Ed.) 2015, *History and Philology*, Associated Regional Chronologies for the Ancient Near East and the Eastern Mediterranean, Vol. III, Brepols.

Sarzec E. de & Heuzey, L. (avec le concours de A. Amiaud et de F. Thureau-Dangin) 1884-1912, *Découvertes en Chaldée*, Paris.

Schrakamp, I. 2015, Urukagina und die Geschichte von Lagaš am Ende der präsargonischen Zeit, *It's a Long Way to a Historiography of the Early Dynastic Period(s)*, R. Dittman and G. Selz (Ed.), p. 303-386.

Selz, G. 1995, *Untersuchungen zur Götterwelt des altsumerischen Staates von Lagaš*, Philadelphia.

— 1998, Über Mesopotamische Herrscaftskonzepte, in *Dubsar anta-men, Festschrift für W. Römer*, Dietrich, M. & Loretz, O. (Eds.), Munster, p. 281-344.

— (with the collaboration of D. Niedermayer) 2015, The Burials After the Battle. Combining Textual and Visual Evidence, *It's a Long Way to a Historiography of the Early Dynastic Period(s)*, R. Dittman and G. Selz (Ed.), p. 387-404.

Sollberger, E. 1959, La frontière de Šara, *Orientalia* 28, p. 336-350.

Steiner, G. 1986, Der Grenzvertrag zwischen Lagaš und Umma, *Acta Sumerologica* 8, p. 219-300.

Steinkeller, P. 1992, Mesopotamia in the Third Millennium BC, *Anchor Bible Dictionary* 4, p. 724-732.

— 1993, Early Political Development in Mesopotamia and the Origins of the Sargonic Empire, *Akkad. The First World Empire. Structure, Ideology, Traditions* , M. Liverani (Ed.), p. 107-129

— 2007, City and Countryside in Third Millennium Southern Babylonia, *Settlement and Society: Essays Dedicated to Robert McCormick Adams*, E. Stone (Ed.), p. 185-211.

— 2013, An Archaic 'Prisoner Plaque' from Kiš, *Revue d'Assyriologie*, p. 131-157.

Testart, A. 2004, *La Servitude volontaire*, 1. Les morts d'accompagnement ; 2. L'origine de l'État, Paris.

Westenholz, A. 2002, The Sumerian City-State, *A Comparative Study of Six City-State Cultures*, M. Hansen (Ed.), Copenhagen.

Wilkinson, T. 2003, *Archaeological Landscapes of the Near East*, Tucson: University of Arizona Press.

— 2013, Hydraulic Landscapes and Irrigation Systems of Sumer, *The Sumerian World*, H. Crawford (Ed.), p. 33-54.

Wittfogel, K. 1957, *Oriental Despotism. A Comparative Study of Total Power*, New Haven & London.